Soutl

GW00806376

To you

for new Adventures,
have a wonderful
time!

Love Marie-Thérèse

christmas 2007.

A guide to recent architecture

...

Christina Muwanga

South Africa

A guide to recent architecture

● ● ● ellipsis KÖNEMANN

• • •

CREATED, EDITED AND DESIGNED BY
Ellipsis London Limited
2 Rufus Street London N1 6PE
E MAIL ...@ellipsis.co.uk
www http://www.ellipsis.com
PUBLISHED IN THE UK AND AFRICA BY
Ellipsis London Limited
SERIES EDITOR Tom Neville
EDITOR Jane Lamacraft
SERIES DESIGN Jonathan Moberly
SUPPORTED BY PFG Building Glass and Alpha (Uganda) Ltd

COPYRIGHT © 1998 Könemann
Verlagsgesellschaft mbH
Bonner Straße 126, D-50968 Köln
PRODUCTION MANAGER Detlev Schaper
PRINTING AND BINDING Sing Cheong
Printing Ltd
Printed in Hong Kong

ISBN 3 8290 0476 1 (Könemann)
ISBN 1 899858 56 3 (Ellipsis)

Christina Muwanga 1998

Contents

Introduction

Containing more than 100 projects, most designed within the last ten years, this guidebook offers a snapshot of South African architecture at a particular time. Its aim is to give an insight into the various social, political and economic influences that have moulded recent work. The projects are drawn from the urban centres and the surrounding areas of South Africa's three main provinces: Gauteng (Johannesburg), KwaZulu-Natal (Durban) and Western Cape (Cape Town).

At the time of writing, South Africa was only three years into democracy. The time frame of this book encompasses a period of political transition within a bleak economic climate. The last thirty years have been marked by deep economic recession – partly in concert with the international condition, but more particularly as a result of the political situation in South Africa. Serious unrest in a country in the throes of reform and change was exacerbated by international economic sanctions and disinvestment. For the architectural profession, the economic and political vicissitudes of this time brought austerity and, with the advent of democracy, the opportunity to transform itself as it comes to terms with and attempts to address its cultural heritage.

From the time of European colonisation more than 300 years ago, the fabric of South African cities has never been free of racial considerations. Urban centres have traditionally been the domain of the white population with development following architectural styles and influences drawn from their countries of origin. The country's more recent political history, forty years of apartheid, with its racist legislation and structures of separate development, made it impossible for architecture to be an autonomous apolitical activity. The cultural barometer that is architecture expresses these factors. Yet, perversely, the neglect of indigenous traditions, the social engineering and reality distortions of apartheid with the resulting exclusivity of the architectural profession mean that no representation of recent work can be a true reflection of South African society. This is seen in the fact that in a country where more than 80 per cent of the population is black, this majority constitutes less than 2 per cent of registered architects.

South Africa presents an extreme juxtaposition of poverty and wealth. The choice of projects in this book attempts to reflect this by cutting a swathe across the disparate environments in which the country's architects are practising and their wide range of concerns: from the aspirations of corporate and institutional clients in central business districts to addressing basic needs of communities in township and rural areas. Much of the work of architects practising in underdeveloped environments is ultimately about process – a move from prescriptive rules to participatory bargaining. The intensity of commitment required for this kind of work demands a redefinition of the traditional role of the architect. Buildings are not merely finished objects but the outcome of complex, inclusive processes that have ramifications beyond the normal sphere of architectural activity. At the other end of the scale, work in the inner cities presents the extreme opposite: commodification of space in a developer-driven building industry. The lull in major construction during the last decade combined with the deregulation of statuary fees has fostered cut-throat competition in which working at risk (a situation whereby the remuneration is contingent on the project actually going ahead) for property developers has become entrenched in the profession.

The prosperity of the mid-1960s showed a different picture. Foreign architects were commissioned to design major buildings, mainly in Johannesburg. Among these is the monumental Carlton Centre (1966–72; Skidmore, Owings and Merrill) constructed on a superblock assembly of five city blocks, and the Standard Bank building (1971; Hentrich & Pettsnich) distinguished by its innovative structural design. During South Africa's isolation virtually no international practices (with the high-profile exception of Chicago-based Murphy/Jahn) have made their mark on the country's cities. Nonetheless, the wide range of approaches witnessed in recent work has tended to replicate international concerns: replication of the past, neo-classicism (deconstructivism has generally stayed on students' drawing boards) and the excesses of post-modernism, a phase which appears to have brought in its wake a view that anything goes. Stylistically, references have been made to a variety of different sources from Victorian mansions to Ndebele vernacular to European rationalism. Amidst the faddish regurgitations or the simply downright strange, there is an increasing body of work by, among others, Roelof Uytenbogaardt, Paul Mikula and Jo Noero which reflects architects' search for regional meaning and form.

South Africa is vast. Cape Town, Johannesburg and Durban, because of their historical development and relative positions within this country, present awesome diversity: the physical landscape of Gauteng of featureless grassland, modest natural ridges and imposing golden dumps of mine-waste; Durban's lush subtropical environment and the predominantly Mediterranean climate of the Cape.

Known as the 'Mother City', Cape Town is the oldest urban area in South Africa. It is the country's most cosmopolitan city which, with its stunning location, is already becoming one of the world's most fashionable tourist destinations. Established in 1652, Cape Town is characterised by the historic influence of Dutch settlers and Victorian English rulers. Johannesburg, born of unbridled commercialism, is the archetypal Boomtown. By the 1970s the city's central area had been almost rebuilt three times, expressing the booms of 1908, 1936 and the 1950s. Its finely grained city grid (originating from the formalisation of nineteenth-century mining camps) offers a unique urban experience in Africa. It is South Africa's most important economic centre at the heart of the most populous and prosperous urban agglomeration in the subcontinent, the Witswatersrand. Durban is the city with the most distinctly African feel. It is South Africa's second-largest urban centre and, because of its proximately to the national economic heartland, it also ranks as South Africa's second-most-important centre of economic growth.

Yet despite their dramatic differences, all the cities are bound by the indelible stamp of apartheid. Impervious to the repeal of legislation that has greatly changed South African society, the built environment remains the most concrete manifestation of four decades of apartheid. No other country has embarked on so thorough a reorganisation of its urban space for the purpose of segregation. A basic knowledge of the structure of the 'Apartheid City' is essential in understanding why South African cities appear as they do. All have been affected by past government policy, most profoundly by the draconian legislation of the Group Areas Act (1950), the cornerstone of apartheid, which radically altered their social and physical character. Generally, the inner city and its surrounding suburbs were proclaimed exclusively white areas. Other racial groups were consigned to the periphery within isolated, racially zoned neighbourhoods. Physical separation between groups was further entrenched by buffer strips either of major road and rail infrastructure or simply vast tracks of vacant land within which regional facilities such as hospitals, military camps and sewerage works were located. The imposition of such negative planning, in conjunction with the state's housing policy, has as its legacy divided cities with township (peripheral neighbourhood) areas characterised by sprawling undifferentiated urban landscapes. The limited or non-existent social and commercial infrastructure in these areas has had severe social and economic consequences.

The challenge to city planners and designers in post-apartheid South Africa is clearly set out in the African National Congress' Reconstruction and Development Programme (RDP). For the first time since the Freedom Charter of 1955, a document outlining a programme of reversing the policies of the past was available to guide planners. At its heart was the stated desire to 'democratise society'. At the time of writing, proposals seeking ways in which its political objectives translate into innovative planning solutions were still very much in the pipeline. Recently approved, one of the first such strategies to be approved is Urban Solution's Baralink Development Framework, the proposed development of 15,000 hectares of vacant land between Soweto (SOuth WEstern TOwnships) and Johannesburg. Its aim is to facilitate meeting basic needs while integrating segregated townships back into the fabric of the city.

While planners and politicians try to negotiate red tape and financing respectively, vacant land throughout the country has been subject to systematic land invasion, with informal settlers appropriating plots and erecting makeshift dwellings in settlements on the city periphery. This situation is indicative of the housing crisis in South Africa; the government is currently faced with a huge backlog, escalating demand and limited resources. In the grand apartheid plan, housing was a powerful mechanism of social engineering and the township with its NE 51 series of houses was regarded as the ideal solution. Contrary to the object-oriented approach of that period, the emphasis of recent housing programmes is on process-oriented delivery (geared towards access to delivery procedures, financing mechanisms and user needs). The basic model is usually the free-standing, single-storey unit. This failure to tackle process and product simultaneously has resulted in the same urban sprawl. New schemes, such as Blue Downs and Delft in Cape Town, reflect the same features: bleak landscapes covered in a non-differentiated blanket of free-standing little boxes. Not all the planned social infra-structures can be provided.

In the inner city the most influential development trend, with its greatest impact on Johannesburg, has been that of decentralisation. The economic situation brought about a huge upsurge in suburban develop-ments, smaller and lower-risk than city-centre schemes. A mass relocation of businesses followed, fleeing the 'crime and grime' image of Johannes-burg CBD for the greener pastures of numerous exotically named mani-cured-lawned office parks and rezoned former residential locations. There are, however, many notable exceptions to this decentralisation, including Meyer Pienaar's Reserve Bank and Revel Fox's enormous BankCity development, the country's two most controversial projects.

Still in its embryonic stage, the redevelopment of the Newtown area bordering the Johannesburg CBD offers a potential catalyst not only to rejuvenate the ramshackle CBD but also to define the role which Johan-nesburg is to play in the Southern Africa of the next century. Formerly the Municipal Electricity premises, the area's conglomeration of buildings is in the process of being converted into what is hoped will become a cultural precinct accommodating a range of art and entertainment venues as well as community-based enterprises.

Durban and Cape Town have both experienced successful urban rede-velopment programmes: the phenomenally successful Victoria & Alfred Waterfront, the redevelopment of Cape Town's industrial dockland area; and

South Africa: a guide to recent architecture

in Durban the development of the Centrum, a 28-hectare site made available for development when the railways ceased to penetrate the city centre in the late 1970s. Both strategies came about as a result of tax laws requiring state departments to pay property tax. In possession of enormous land holdings, the authorities responsible for the railways and harbours had to rationalise their land holdings in order to alleviate their tax obligations (a move that made land available for several smaller-scale projects such as Nyanga Junction, an industrial-style commercial centre by GAPP Architects in Cape Town).

Pre-democracy, the country saw the attrition of public life and buildings as a result of apartheid policy. A great deal of construction took place, largely designed to support apartheid's numerous bureaucratic structures in the cities with bizarre and extravagant complexes built in the semi-independent 'homelands' established under the regime's policy of decentralisation and resettlement. Allocation of public schemes was confined to a select group of architects. In the profession, resistance to the ideologies of the state was manifested in a range of individual stands, from refusal of government work to leaving the country. The most notable challenge to the *status quo* was the formation of Architects Against Apartheid (AAA), an informal pressure group.

Because of the need to redress the inequalities of the past, work in the public sector has seen a number of changes. The most controversial is in the roster system where an affirmative-action policy (with a bias towards previously marginalised groups) has been applied to the allocation of public work. Underdeveloped areas have been a particular focus, resulting in a range of 'upliftment' strategies providing facilities such as clinics, schools and sporting venues. Sport is very important in South African culture and one of the few aspects of South African life that crosses the racial divide. With 60 per cent of the country's youth active participants in sport, it clearly has a potential in youth development, and indeed in nation building. For many, hosting and winning the 1995 rugby World Cup is the most poignant symbol of South Africa's new democracy and reacceptance into the international community.

Several projects have come about as a result of South Africa's bid to host the 2004 Olympic Games. Though ultimately unsuccessful, one achievement of the bid effort was that it united the country's architects in a spirit of open competition with a common goal. It is perhaps this alliance that promises the answer to the challenge of the new millennium: for architects and planners in South Africa to wield their power towards a synthesising vision of collective life; to make architecture and cities that can at once reflect, celebrate and inspire all the people of this diverse nation.

South Africa: a guide to recent architecture

Using this book

This guide is divided into three sections: Cape Town (Western Cape), Johannesburg (Gauteng), and Durban (KwaZulu-Natal), with their respective entries grouped in sections for the various areas of the cities and their surrounds. Listed after the address of most projects are co-ordinates from the most recent editions of MapStudio's A–Z street maps of each city indicating the exact location.

The public transport system in South Africa is a combination of formal and informal services that are generally erratic and can be confusing for visitors. So, while central areas can generally be covered on foot, a car is invaluable for visits to projects outside the city centres. In these instances directions have been provided; these assume the trip is starting from the centre of town. Where appropriate references have also been made to more reliable and easy-to-use transport services such as the train system in Cape Town and Myrnah buses in Durban.

For visitors to the cities, personal security should be a prime consideration. I would recommend that journeys be planned so that you are aware of the precise location of the project you intend to visit and how to get to it before setting off. Particular care should be taken in arranging trips to sites in central Johannesburg and township areas in general. If possible you should arrange to be accompanied by someone familiar with the area. If this is not possible, for visits to Johannesburg CBD I suggest you contact the Johannesburg Publicity Association (011 337 3266) for advice or to arrange for an escort. In the case of visits to projects in township areas you could contact the relevant architects who may be able to advise you.

ACKNOWLEDGEMENTS

I would like to thank all the architects for the time they spent showing me around their projects, answering my questions and for all the documentation they supplied; the architecture faculty of the University of the Witswatersrand for use of their office and library facilities during my research in Johannesburg; for their hospitality Desiree Smith and André Koekemoer (Johannesburg), Paul Mikula, Roz and Rodney Harber (Durban), Gita Goven and Alastair Rendall (Cape Town); Gideon Scott, Johan Jacobs, Nina Saunders, Andrew Makin, Tim Laubinger for their encouragement and support; special thanks to Andreas Werner for his help, photography and for making it possible for me to complete the documentation of this guide based in South Africa; and to Tom Neville and Jonathan Moberly for the opportunity to participate in this guide series.

This book is dedicated to my mother Kasalina and my late father Paulo Muwanga.

CT December 1997

PUBLISHER'S NOTE

The publisher would like to thank PFG Building Glass (Pty) Ltd and Alpha (Uganda) Ltd for their support.

South Africa: a guide to recent architecture

Central Cape Town

House Back

This house clearly reads as two interrelated but separate sections. The first is a double-storey cubic wing of quasi-cellular service spaces with window openings giving selected views. The second, by contrast, is uncluttered and expansive – a vast terrace at entry level with open-plan living and dining areas enjoying panoramic views of the city below.

The narrow space between the sections both connects the wings and emphasises their separateness: a naturally lit, double-volume circulation spine containing the principal stairway and a bridge is edged by a powerful wall element which slices through the building.

Once penetrated, the entrance – a massive plane filling the slot – presents visitors with a dazzling swathe through the city, framed by the slot's glazed open end. To the side, a glazed passage link beyond the spine wall provides access to the roof terrace and a bridge across the slot to the main bedroom. Some 5 metres below, the transparent living areas are afforded shade and privacy by an ingenious set of remote-control sunscreens constructed by a yacht builder from perforated aluminium more commonly used in the mining industry to sift mined earth. From the outside, the screens appear transparent or opaque, depending on the time of day or the mood of the occupant. The space inside is delineated by structural steel columns which, emerging through the roof slab, anchor on to the spine wall to form a crate-like frame over the terrace above.

ADDRESS 1 Hildene Road, Tamboerskloof
CLIENTS Oliver and Krysia Back
STRUCTURAL ENGINEER Henry Fagan & Partners
SIZE 300 square metres
GETTING THERE Adderley to Kloof Nek bus (bus stop no. 73)
ACCESS none

Central Cape Town

Architects van der Merwe Miszewski 1996

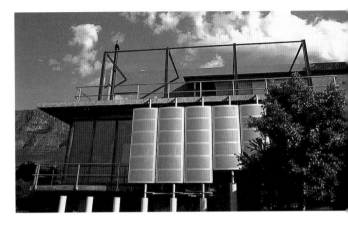

Central Cape Town

Architects van der Merwe Miszewski 1996

Longkloof Studios

Something of a landmark in the mainly residential Gardens area, the Longkloof 'Tower' advertises a successful redevelopment of a derelict city-bowl industrial site. The buildings – a conglomeration of turn-of-the-century factories, warehouses and offices once used by the United Tobacco Company – feature façade treatments influenced by the arts and crafts movement. The first building, an industrial warehouse by Jones & McWilliams, was specially designed for the needs of the tobacco industry.

In 1993 the Cape Provincial Administration decided to hold a proposal call for architect/developer teams to upgrade the run-down fabric of the site. Proposals varied from total demolition to more sensitive approaches. The scheme that was eventually chosen provided the opportunity to integrate the large site back into the historically sensitive area while at the same time creating a link with the upper Gardens area and the city itself.

Today the Longkloof development acts as a kind of media centre, housing tenant companies which are mainly involved in television or advertising.

Central Cape Town

ADDRESS Darter's Road, Gardens
ASSOCIATE ARCHITECT Samuel Pauw Architects
GETTING THERE Kloof Street towards Table Mountain; take the first turning to your right
ACCESS public areas open

ARX II Architects 1993

ARX II Architects 1993

CPA Headquarters

Within an urban context characterised by quaint Victorian and apologetic modern buildings, the CPA headquarters is the architectural equivalent of a slap in the face. The architects have successfully transformed an awkward brief – an office building with no major spaces and no street-related uses – into a solid and sensitive work. It is a concrete modernist building and makes no bones about it – the aesthetic is grey, tough and uncompromising. Nine storeys high, the building dominates a typical city block. The impact of its bulk on Long Street's predominantly two- and three-storey historic buildings is lessened by a narrow band of retained existing buildings.

The project's most striking feature is its innovative use of concrete. A system of angled sunscreens (*in situ* vertical and precast horizontal concrete fins varying in size and inclination) shields the office levels on the east, west and north façades. The deep, carefully proportioned *brise-soleil* lightens the form of the building, creating intense, varying patterns of light and shade while its edges are softened by corner balconies.

Central Cape Town

ADDRESS 9 Dorp Street
CLIENT Cape Provincial Administration
STRUCTURAL ENGINEER K F D Wilkinson & Partners
CONTRACT VALUE R14.7 million
SIZE 20,078 square metres
ACCESS restricted to entrance courtyard

Revel Fox & Partners 1984

Central Cape Town

Revel Fox & Partners 1984

Protea Assurance Building

Headquarters to the Protea Assurance company for more than half a century, this Cape Town landmark has been upgraded and extended to provide additional office space. The building faces on to the historically protected area of Greenmarket Square – a leafy cobblestoned expanse jammed with market stalls during the day and boasting a number of interesting buildings including the City Hall. On another side, the building overlooks the hustle and bustle of St George's Mall, Cape Town's main commercial corridor.

Completed in 1939, the original building is an interesting and quirky collage of styles. Rising from a distinctly neo-classical base – all Doric columns and moulded cornices – it gradually gives way to art deco undercurrents to complete its style mutation in the pure geometry of an arched gable. The demolition of adjacent buildings made space for an addition which, L-shaped in plan, extends the original building's two near-identical façades (looking on to Greenmarket Square and St George's Street) by 12 and 30 metres respectively and in two completely different styles.

The challenge for the architects was to design extensions that would be harmonious with, yet distinct from, the rigid symmetry of the old façades, without giving a lopsided impression overall. Most successful is the Greenmarket Square frontage, where the extension provides a new entrance and service core (the old core was removed to form an atrium space). Here, in deference to the sensitive context and limited space, the detailing refers to that of the original building. However, this is far from slavish mimicry. Some of the older decorative themes such as plaster mouldings are selectively reintroduced to give cohesion and, like its older counterpart, the extension is finished in dazzling white-painted plaster.

Rather than jostle for attention with the bold, protruding elements that mark the old entrance, the new entrance accomplishes a subtle finishing

Louis Karol Architects 1990

Central Cape Town

Louis Karol Architects 1990

stroke with its central feature – a wide recess running from the third floor to the roof, flanked up to the fifth floor by two circular columns. The gesture bestows the new entrance with grandeur and distinction while establishing an equilibrium between façades old and new.

The façade on the St George's Street side of the building is less successful. With more room to manoeuvre, the architects have opted for a clear departure from the style of the original, ditching some critical clues in the process. In response to the context, the language and detailing here are more modern, simplified and abstracted, with a 6-metre-wide 'pause' section of curtain-walling dividing the new from the old. Instead of a recess, the main feature is a 13-metre-wide bow to the façade, with a window balcony (apparently simulating one on the original Protea building façade) that manages to look incongruous and forlorn. The plaster mouldings have been dispensed with, leaving large unbroken expanses of plaster to show up the unevenness of the workmanship and generally magnify any building defects.

ADDRESS Greenmarket Square
CLIENT Protea Assurance
STRUCTURAL ENGINEER Louis Karol Structural, Les Vides
CONTRACT VALUE R15 million
SIZE 9,720 square metres
ACCESS none

Louis Karol Architects 1990

Louis Karol Architects 1990

SRG House

The new offices of the Select Retail Group (SRG), the country's largest fashion chain, are on a high-profile site just behind City Hall. (The company's main headquarters occupy the massive Wooltru House development situated diagonally opposite, also by Roberts & Loebenberg.)

The building is composed of three horizontal segments, of which only the uppermost is occupied by SRG offices. The middle of the 'sandwich' accommodates lettable space and corporate facilities in a section characterised by curved edges. Seemingly compressed, this segment bulges outwards, inflated by rings of angled sunscreen visors. At street level there is retail space and an entrance foyer, with parking above.

Inside, energy efficiency has been a consideration: two four-storey glazed atrium spaces act as the building's lungs, dispelling rising hot air through controlled louvres so that excessive heat is eliminated in summer and passive heat encouraged in winter. The atrium spaces also encourage the free flow of communication within the building, with the larger one providing a focus for the SRG levels. Here, the space is enlivened by generous planting, curved galleries and bridge links to exposed stairways.

Bounded by relatively narrow side streets, the building's segmentation, street-level retail space and large setback provide relief to what would otherwise have been an overwhelming mass.

ADDRESS 1 Mostert Street
CLIENT Wooltru Properties
STRUCTURAL ENGINEER B S Bergman & Partners Inc.
CONTRACT VALUE R62 million
SIZE 41,119 square metres
ACCESS none

Roberts & Loebenberg 1995

Central Cape Town

Roberts & Loebenberg 1995

Safmarine House

Safmarine House started life as 'Sea Street', taking its name from the street that once crossed its city-block site from Strand Street to the sea (this is an area of reclaimed land). Mid-contract, the Safmarine shipping corporation decided to take more than half the building, and with it the naming rights. The subsequent name change was apt, since prior to construction archaeological digs on the site had yielded items ferried across the seas by the corporation's distant predecessors.

Starting from a brief that called for an 'environmentally friendly building', the architects developed a cruciform plan which provided shallow office space, operable windows, natural light and views. With a convoluted façade spanning 53.5 metres from wing tip to wing tip, this 23-storey tower handles its bulk with surprising lightness. Careful articulation of the wings, as well as their differentiation from the main shaft through window treatment and colouring, gives the impression of a more slenderly proportioned building. The tower terminates in a geometric interplay of a pyramid held within a framed cube.

The tower's podium is surrounded by a covered colonnade which gives a human scale to the building and marks the entrance with an exuberant crescent lined with palm trees. Panelled in pink beech with parquet flooring, the foyer glows with warmth, making a welcome change from the chilly granite and marble routinely found in corporate foyers.

ADDRESS 22 Riebeek Street
CLIENT Old Mutual Properties
STRUCTURAL ENGINEER Ove Arup Inc.
CONTRACT VALUE R72.5 million
SIZE 40,000 square metres
ACCESS restricted to certain floors

Central Cape Town

Louis Karol Architects 1993

Central Cape Town

Louis Karol Architects 1993

The Terraces

This speculative office development occupies a city block and comprises a tower, a low block and a glazed link. Rarely seen as a whole, the relative volumes of the tower and its Waterkant Street frontage present an extreme juxtaposition of scale arising from the wish to retain a measure of historical context while achieving the desired commercial returns.

The tower evidently gains its name from its sea-facing terraced profile, which provides offices on its upper storeys with narrow verandah-like enclosures from which to enjoy the view. Four corner turrets, shrouded in a reflecting glass wall of ambiguous height and capped by glass pyramids, provide further interest to the upper levels. However, all this gesturing cannot distract from the disastrous treatment at ground level.

Scaled to the height of its neighbours, a three-storey plinth given over entirely to parking creates a hostile pedestrian environment and at the same time breaks up the continuity of shopping and other street activities. A ponderous entrance portico obscures rather than highlights the pivotal role of the glazed entrance court as the seam between the building and its adjoining premises. The latter accommodates large studio spaces, inserted behind the adjacent row of Victorian buildings of which only the façades are retained. The tower is finished in a horizontal banded masonry which, combined with pink glazing, gives a warm glow.

Central Cape Town

ADDRESS corner Bree and Waterkant Streets
CLIENT Equikor
STUCTURAL ENGINEER Sonnekus & Toerien
CONTRACT VALUE R23.3 million
SIZE 16,950 square metres
ACCESS none

Munnik Visser Black Fish & Partners 1992

Central Cape Town

Munnik Visser Black Fish & Partners 1992

BP Centre

The BP Centre is Cape Town's tallest building. Twisted at a 45-degree to the rectangular city grid, the 32-storey tower stands on a site enclosing the northern corner of Thibault Square, a large, underused public space. The tower's shift against the grain serves the dual function of reducing sun load and providing occupants with improved mountain and seascape views. However, this building's enduring landmark status owes as much to the simple monumentality of its design as to its distinctive height and orientation.

A square with rounded corners in plan, the tower is supported minimally by eight circular perimeter columns and a central service core – an arrangement integral to its overall aesthetic. At ground level the structure is exposed by an invitingly transparent double-volume foyer contained within a suspended, frameless glass drum. The façades consist of the columns, beam liners and concrete sunscreens which, set slightly away from the building, shield its east, north and west elevations. All finished in an aggregate of dark-grey stone, these appear like a crusty exoskeleton protecting the continuous full-height glazing of each office floor.

A bridge links the tower to a low-rise building housing BP's public relations facilities as well as public amenities at ground level. This two-storey building also shields the square's pedestrian area from the heavy traffic.

ADDRESS Thibault Square
CLIENT Mine Officials Pension Fund
STRUCTURAL ENGINEER Ove Arup & Partners
CONTRACT VALUE R8.5 million
SIZE 35,000 square metres
ACCESS limited to certain floors

Revel Fox & Partners 1972

Revel Fox & Partners 1972

Victoria Junction complex

At the time this complex was built, Cape Town was experiencing a boom in loft conversions. The trend for loft living as a 'lifestyle' statement has changed the face of the city as the truly trendy have traded in their GASH (Good Area Small Home) cluster of rooms in suburbia for cubic metres in the Central Business District.

Located between the city centre and the Victoria & Alfred Waterfront Development (see page 40), Victoria Junction is a mixed-use complex occupying a city block of approximately 16,000 square metres. The site was previously occupied by a group of low-level buildings housing Green Point's telephone works. The development consists of four phases ranging from the refurbishment of two existing industrial buildings to a completely new office and loft development and a hotel.

In the patchwork fabric of its surroundings, the development is an island of consistency, with new additions supporting the industrial ethos of the existing buildings. Inside is a series of internal courts, hermetically sealed from the city by a wall of perimeter buildings. The lofts feature mezzanine levels in high volumes, rough facebrick and sealed skim for walls, screed and timber for floors, and exposed steelwork. A strong communal atmosphere pervades the complex.

ADDRESS Victoria Junction, Ebenezer Road, Green Point
CLIENT Newport Property Group
STRUCTURAL ENGINEER Gadomski Partnership
CONTRACT VALUE R35.5 million
GETTING THERE from the CBD take Green Point Main Road. Turn right after the Victoria Junction Hotel.
ACCESS public areas open

Central Cape Town

KCVR Architects 1996

KCVR Architects 1996

Victoria Junction Hotel

'Hey, you in the 4 x 4, this is for you!' The hoarding that appeared outside this hotel during construction basically sums it up. A spin-off of the loft apartment concept, it is aimed at a young, creative market, particularly the international film and advertising crews who are increasingly using the city as a location.

Visually a cornerstone to the Victoria Junction complex (see page 36), the building is clearly visible from the Sea Point approach, which means that it is also seen as the gateway to the city centre. An L-shaped plan abutting the street gives rise to façades articulated to lead the eye around the corner. The momentum is set at ground level by a curved projection containing a restaurant and administration facilities, reinforced by balconies on the levels above. The wings of the building provide a rib-like modular backdrop to this gesture, established by plastered piers leading into fins supporting the deep eaves structure. The overhang and fins provide shade and privacy for the loft apartments, which are differentiated from hotel rooms by full-height glazing. The main entrance is off the side road and round the back of the hotel. Its curious location arose because of the need to retain an existing stone perimeter wall protected by the National Monuments Council (the body responsible for protecting and conserving sites of architectural interest in South Africa).

ADDRESS corner Somerset and Ebenezer Roads, Green Point
CLIENT Newport Property Group
STRUCTURAL ENGINEER Gadomski Partnership
CONTRACT VALUE R25 million
SIZE 11,270 square metres
GETTING THERE Green Point Main Road
ACCESS open

Central Cape Town

KCVR Architects 1996

Central Cape Town

KCVR Architects 1996

Victoria & Alfred Waterfront Development

The establishment of the Victoria & Alfred Waterfront Company in 1988 heralded the start of a public sector initiative to attract investment back into the underdeveloped and partly redundant industrial dockland area of Cape Town. The area is located on the Atlantic seaboard, close to the city centre and southern suburbs, yet its historical development has been functionally and physically separate from the city and its residents. (From the 1940s, the city's waterfront was strictly controlled by the South African Railway and Harbours, with access allowed only to dockworkers, fishermen and harbour personnel.)

The masterplan follows the blueprint set by successful international precedents. The insertion of tourist-related infrastructure and retail, hotel and office facilities has been coupled with an enthusiastic adoption of the style-and-form template which makes 'the waterfront experience' almost identical across the world.

While components common to their port sites – warehouses, sheds, quays, cranes, bollards and so on – bind dockland developments all around the world, here, unlike other models, tourist elements sit alongside the traditional working harbour. This is the scheme's winning card. The ambience is set by the sights, sounds and smells of a real harbour, and old buildings have been conserved wherever possible (though in some cases you would need a trained eye to discern new from old, such is the overly reverent effort made to blend in the new additions).

Visitors can experience a squeaky clean, romanticised reconstruction of the past: quaint wooden promenades, wrought-iron and wooden street furniture and emporium façades invite you to partake in a neo-Victorian life of privileged leisure. The centrepiece is the arched glass and iron galleria of the Victoria Wharf shopping centre, which is carefully styled

1988–

Central Cape Town

1988–

to evoke a Victorian railway station. It is a sanitised Disneyesque world of leisure whose acknowledgement of its unique cultural landscape is limited to the information boards which dot the site – small fragmented images of Cape Town's history overshadowed by the shopping centres.

The precinct is not solely a tourist attraction but also a retail and recreational mecca for Capetonians. With up to 12 million visitors a year, its success compares with that of San Francisco's Pier 39.

In or near the development there are a number of key projects well worth visiting: Victoria Wharf, designed by Louis Karol Architects; the Two Oceans Aquarium, by Dennis Fabian Berman Hackner Architects; the Breakwater Graduate School of Business, by Revel Fox & Partners (see page 44); the BMW Pavilion, by Derick Henstra Architects (see page 46); Quay Four and the NSRI boathouse, and the Portswood Square office complex, both by GAPP Architects & Urban Designers.

ADDRESS Victoria & Alfred Waterfront
DEVELOPER Victoria & Alfred Waterfront (Pty) Ltd
GETTING THERE take the Waterfront bus from Adderley Street (in front of the bus terminal and tourist information centre)
ACCESS open

1988–

1988–

Breakwater Graduate School of Business

Overlooking the Victoria & Alfred docks, the turreted building of the former Breakwater Prison is one of the few remaining monuments to what was, for most of the century, the Colony's largest convict station. Built in 1901 to accommodate white prisoners, the building marked the first structural separation between black and white prisoners who, until that time, had been housed together. Its conversion into the University of Cape Town's graduate school of business formed part of the second phase of the Victoria & Alfred Waterfront Development (see page 40).

The scheme exploits the building's original cloister design to provide offices, a library, lecture halls and seminar rooms in an infill building which occupies most of what was once a vast prison yard – now a clinically landscaped courtyard. On its inner side, overhead bridges connect the new section to the old (its prison cells are now seminar rooms) across a naturally lit internal passage which acts as a continuous seam between the two structures. The prison's external architecture is preserved, flanked by two new buildings: a student residence block which repeats the courtyard format, and an amenities building with hotel accommodation.

ADDRESS Portswood Ridge, Victoria & Alfred Waterfront
CLIENT University of Cape Town
STRUCTURAL ENGINEER K F D Wilkinson & Partners
CONTRACT VALUE R30 million
SIZE 18,850 square metres
GETTING THERE take the Victoria & Alfred Waterfront bus from the tourist information centre in Adderley Street
ACCESS announce yourself

Central Cape Town

Revel Fox & Partners 1991

BMW Pavilion

Designed to promote a more accessible image for the exclusive German car and motorcycle manufacturer, the BMW Pavilion combines a people-friendly programme with a landmark presence at the entrance of the Victoria & Alfred Waterfront Development (see page 40).

Derived from the BMW logo, the building's plan consists of a cylindrical main volume to which the three-storey 'blind-box' of an Imax cinema is added. One of approximately 200 Imax cinemas worldwide, this has a 15-metre screen and state-of-the-art technology, making it without doubt the main attraction among the competing amenities – bistro, exhibition space and so on – which occupy the five-storey building's ground floor. The radial layout rigidly applied to upper office and conference levels here becomes an open-plan public core, with spaces loosely defined by floor levels and curved wall fragments. A continuous glass wall displays the various activities within. The quality of accessibility (be it only visual) is reflected throughout the design, which allows tantalising glimpses into no-go areas such as the cinema projection room.

There are two entrances to the building, with restraint on the city façade giving way to more elaborate articulation on the 'soft' waterfront elevation. The architects' modern handling provides a refreshing antidote to the cloying sweetness of the surrounding 'Victoriana'.

ADDRESS Victoria & Alfred Waterfront
CLIENT BMW SA (Pty) Ltd
STRUCTURAL ENGINEER Henry Fagan & Partners
CONTRACT VALUE R14 million
GETTING THERE take the Victoria & Alfred Waterfront bus from the tourist information centre in Adderley Street
ACCESS public areas open

Central Cape Town

Derrick Henstra Architects 1994

Derrick Henstra Architects 1994

Cape Town suburbs

House Contursi

The brief for this building, which is situated on the slopes of Lion's Head, was to alter the two lower levels of an existing house and turn its upper floor into an 'entertainment space', making the most of the spectacular 360-degree views. The result is a double curved roof whose shell-like form lifts to capture the varying mountain views at the entrance and extends into an enclosing overhang shading the exposed sea-facing side of the house.

Inside, open-plan living areas are interposed with curved wall fragments, reinforcing the project's sensual character. The nearby coast provides the inspiration for the choice of materials: white cement, cretestone, limewashed timber and sand-coloured stone. Seats and ledges, cast *in situ*, form part of the sculptural whole.

Cape Town suburbs

ADDRESS 7 Clifton Road, Clifton
CLIENT Enzo Contursi
STRUCTURAL ENGINEER Abacus
Consulting Engineers
SIZE 480 square metres
GETTING THERE take Kloof Nek
Road towards Table Mountain.
Turn right into Kloof Road, then
take the first turning on your
right into Clifton Road
ACCESS none

Stefan Antoni Architects 1997

Stefan Antoni Architects 1997

House Fagan

A seminal work, this house is the architect's own home, which he and his family built over weekends and during their spare time. Set back behind a sunken court, it turns its back to the severe south-east winds that rake its coastal site, commanding a dazzling view over a nature reserve to the Atlantic Ocean and the horizon.

It has a simple yet striking silhouette. An undulating profiled roof echoes the movement of distant waves while the exaggerated chimney of a protruding fireplace provides a static counterfoil to the roof's motion.

The careful detailing and choice of materials elevate the modest entrance to an experiential sequence that draws you into the house. From the elevated car port with its grille wall, stone steps funnel downwards, becoming narrower as they lead towards the heavy copper-sheathed main door. From the bottom of the stairs, the floor changes texture to become dimpled, inlaid with round river stone, channelling you downwards along a narrow ramping passage of gradually increasing height. Approaching the core of the house the passage width swells below a circular skylight to become a raised timber deck protruding into the living room. Here you are confronted for the first time by the magnificent view. Twenty metres of living space stretch either side of you, with one wall made of four full-height sliding glass doors. Even when these doors are closed, the impression is of the room being an open deck poised above the sea, its interior space a continuation of the surrounding landscape. Nestled in the centre of the opposite wall is the heart of the house – a massive fireplace with a sunken seating area embraced by the hearth.

A flight of suspended treads leads from the platform to the private domain of the bedrooms above. The stairway is screened by steel bars which provide its support and pierce the concrete ceiling slab to become balustrade supports on the upper landing. The first floor accommodates

Gabriel Fagan Architects 1965

Gabriel Fagan Architects 1965

four cellular bedrooms organised symmetrically around two bathrooms. The arrangement complements the ingenious roof which was partly inspired by that of Gaudí's workshop at Sagrada Familia. A generous vault shelters each of the bedrooms which, like the living room below, can become open balconies to the sea. The bathrooms are set below the shallow dip of the roof and enjoy views of the mountain top.

ADDRESS Die Es, 32 Woodford Avenue, Camps Bay
CLIENTS Gabriel and Gwen Fagan
SIZE 329 square metres
GETTING THERE from Cape Town CBD take Kloof Nek Road towards Table Mountain. Kloof Nek Road becomes M62 (Camps Bay); take third turning to your right
ACCESS by appointment (telephone Gabriel Fagan on 021 242 470)

Gabriel Fagan Architects 1965

Gabriel Fagan Architects 1965

Hout Bay Library

Set amid jostling commercial developments, the site of this small library was part of an urban design strategy aimed at integrating the area's buildings and parking lots through a sequence of planted courts. The library, with its treed forecourt and access link from the adjacent shopping centre, echoes the arrangement on a smaller scale.

The building's façade is characterised by a low oversailing roof shading a continuous band of windows. A recessed entrance, overlooked by the librarians' offices, leads through to a lobby providing access to a multipurpose hall, kitchen, staff facilities and the main library space. This is the antithesis of the suburban library stereotype: the public area is a light-filled, loosely defined landscape of spaces. The main feature is the splayed fan-like timber structure supporting the sloping clerestoried roof.

Materials are simple and economical – corrugated iron, bagged white walls with red quarry tiles and various grades of timber. Detailing is carefully considered and inventive, resulting in fully integrated elements – the floor becomes a column base, the column becomes a roof structure, the roof becomes fenestration… A whole greater than the sum of its parts.

ADDRESS Melkhout Crescent, Hout Bay
CLIENT Regional Services Council
CONTRACT VALUE R2 million
SIZE 720 square metres
GETTING THERE take the M6 towards Hout Bay. After the Princess Street turn-off from the Main Road, take the second turning to your right into The Promenade. Take the second turning to your right again into Melkhout Crescent
ACCESS open Monday to Thursday 9.00–19.00, Friday 9.00–18.00, Saturday 9.00–13.00

Uytenbogaardt & Rozendal Architects and Urban Designers 1989

Uytenbogaardt & Rozendal Architects and Urban Designers 1989

House Bothma

Poised on the upper slopes of Hout Bay, this house has breathtaking views of the sea to the south and the mountain to the north. Because the site is rich in indigenous protected flora, the entire building has been suspended over two outdoor 'rooms' (an arrival court whose thickened walls accommodate utility spaces, and a garden court) resulting in a minimal built footprint.

The main house element is a simple linear steel-frame 'glass-box' structure accommodating open-plan living, dining and kitchen areas. Described by the architect as 'a spatial facilitator for living', it reads internally as a continuous space with rooms defined by sliding partitions. Grey steel and natural timber flooring is used throughout, with large glass sliding doors on the southern side extending the space on to a timber deck which runs the length of the house, connecting the inside with the outside. The clean horizontal line of the communal area is punctuated on the eastern end by three identical timber-clad, double-volume 'bedroom towers'. Each tower houses a play/work space with stairs to a bed deck which has dramatic views of both mountain and sea.

When I asked Scott Johnston whether the image and language of the house could be regarded as essentially Eurocentric, he replied: 'I suppose there is a kind of American or European sophistication to the design, given where I've been working [Vienna] and then coming back to South Africa… However, this house was an attempt to move away from Eurocentricity; it's trying very hard to find a technology that fits appropriately into the daily making of buildings in South Africa. I looked among the available technologies to find what could be made well, quickly and relatively cheaply without importing anything foreign. Everything was made here.'

I also asked Johnston about the use of steel in his building, the fact

Scott Johnston 1994

Scott Johnston 1994

that it is often perceived to be a foreign material, despite South Africa's long-established tradition of steel construction. 'Steel construction is just as humdrum here as it is in western countries. It simply hasn't been used in certain contexts as much as it might have been elsewhere – its home has stayed in the industrial sector. If you extend the construction principles to the rural end of the scale or to the lowest cost structure even at a domestic level, often it's a facilitatory frame situation where materials are nailed, stuck or wrapped around. It's exactly that system that is employed here.

'The sophistication that comes through is that, I suppose, more energy was put into the facilitatory frame than would happen in a cruder situation. That, I think, was the challenge of this project – to use a material which, because it is basically costed per kilogramme, allows a certain complexity in detailing without the usual escalation in cost.'

ADDRESS Stirrup Lane, Hout Bay
CLIENT Michael and Simone Bothma
STRUCTURAL ENGINEER Ove Arup Inc.
SIZE 250 square metres
GETTING THERE take M6 (Victoria Avenue) towards Hout Bay and turn off into Victoria Road; take the first turning to your left into Valley Road and proceed for approximately 1.5 kilometres. At World of Birds wildlife sanctuary turn left into Martingale Avenue (dirt road) and then take the first right into Stirrup Lane. The house is at the end of the cul-de-sac
ACCESS by appointment (telephone Simon Husband on 021 230173)

Cape Town suburbs

Scott Johnston 1994

Scott Johnston 1994

House Uytenbogaardt

Perched on a steeply sloping site, this house appears as an exquisite object in complete harmony with its natural landscape. Because of its perfect symmetry and balanced proportions, the house has a powerful and dignified presence which belies its diminutive scale – its 6 x 8 metre footprint barely disturbs the site. Masonry walls enclosing cool, cavernous bedrooms provide a robust, insular base. By contrast, the glazed upper-level living area is expansive, with sweeping sea views connecting it to the landscape. This section – a timber structure and a delicate roof plane seemingly suspended in mid-air – is a more refined piece of construction, like a piece of furniture or joinery slotted into the masonry shell.

An attendant library/studio at the bottom of the site, also conceived as an independent pavilion, contains the forward thrust of the house by twisting against its axis. It comprises a solid brick box with a terrace above it, the roof acting as a pergola.

ADDRESS 36 Nerina Avenue, Kommetjie
CLIENT Roelof Uytenbogaardt
SIZE 96 square metres
GETTING THERE from Cape Town CBD
take Kommetjie Main Road (M65); turn
right after the hotel into Lighthouse
Road and take the fifth turning on your
left
ACCESS by appointment (telephone
Mariane Uytenbogaardt on
021 783 32323)

Uytenbogaardt & Rozendal Architects and Urban Designers 1989

Uytenbogaardt & Rozendal Architects and Urban Designers 1989

Alphen Community Centre

Located in Constantia Valley, an upmarket residential area in Cape Town's Wine Lands, this project has transformed a hotchpotch of existing elements (a community hall with random additions and alterations, a dreary clinic, parking and pedestrian areas) into an understatedly elegant and cohesive whole. The vocabulary of the scheme consciously reflects the local Cape vernacular. The existing fragments are bound together by the grassy central courtyard with its surrounding colonnade, by the austere white massing of parapets and the low, wide *werf* (farmyard) walls. Deep verandahs mediate between the interior and an exterior hierarchy of informal gathering places delineated by surface treatment: earthy laterite gravel panels set within redbrick surrounds, grass and gravel for the extensively treed car-parking area.

Within the hall and its surrounding spaces, natural rooflighting, wood ceilings and red quarry tiles contrast with the existing bagged white walls and plain ceilings to create a warm, tactile environment. Detailing throughout is simple and rigorous.

With the popularisation of the Cape Dutch style, used and abused *ad nauseam* for everything from shopping malls to office parks nationwide, this modest scheme's generous interpretation of the local vernacular comes as delightful breath of fresh air.

ADDRESS Constantia Main Road, Constantia
CLIENT Constantia Local Council
STRUCTURAL ENGINEER Kantey & Templer
GETTING THERE take the Constantia exit off the Blue Route freeway; this leads directly on to Main Road. The centre is on your right after Alphen Park
ACCESS open

Piet Louw Architects 1993

Cape Town suburbs

Piet Louw Architects 1993

Kirstenbosch Glass House

This glass house provides the special conditions required for indigenous plants which cannot be displayed in the natural environment of the Kirstenbosch Botanical Garden.

Sited outside the main garden and screened by avenues of ficus and camphor trees, the glass house is not an intrusive presence – from within the garden, one catches only occasional glimpses of it. Set against a mountain backdrop, the peaks of the glass roof are shaped to get as much winter sun as possible, while open sides provide natural ventilation.

The enclosure houses four plant groupings, each with different climatic requirements: desert plants, ferns and orchids, afro-montaine and bulbous plants. The larger, central 'botanical cathedral' housing the major arid collection is ringed by circulation which feeds into three smaller 'botanical chapels' at each corner. Hard landscaping is organised according to a spiralling golden triangle whose rising terraces give terrific cycloramic views. A giant baobab takes pride of place at its centre.

Materials include sandstone, sandstone-coloured brick, and protective glass for security screens. The glass roof consists of laminated safety glass with an aluminium sub-frame supported off a steel substructure. The main structural feature is a system of triangular girders, only 900 millimetres deep, spanning the 24 metres of the Arid House.

ADDRESS Kirstenbosch Botanical Garden, Newlands
CLIENT National Botanical Institute
ASSOCIATE ARCHITECT Julian Elliot
STRUCTURAL ENGINEER De Villiers Hulme
CONTRACT VALUE R6 million SIZE 1600 square metres
GETTING THERE via Rhodes Drive from Cape Town
ACCESS open every day between 10.00-16.00

Cape Town suburbs

MLH Architects & Planners 1996

Cape Town suburbs

MLH Architects & Planners 1996

Springfield Terrace

This housing scheme formed part of an initiative for the redevelopment of the District Six area, a once vibrant, multi-racial, inner city area demolished in the 1960s (through the application of the Slums Act, which had come to symbolise apartheid's segregationist policies). Three decades later, the objective of the initiative was two-fold: to contribute to the achievement of racially open urban areas; and to demonstrate how South African cities could be reconstructed to make them more efficient, viable and convenient. Chosen as a pilot project, Springfield Terrace was the first large inner-city infill housing scheme aimed at the lower-middle income market. Its design offers positive lessons in place-making – here, real ideas in built form create a cohesive, enclosed public environment for the benefit of inhabitants.

Backing on to the N2 highway, the scheme consists of nine blocks of three- and four-storeys. Densities are deliberately high but because of the generosity of the public areas the overall feeling is spatially loose. A thematic continuity is established not only by the modulation of façades through a pattern of tinted stippled plaster but also by the system of vertical fenestration and the projection of staircases thrusting into the street space. An attic solution to the top storey reduces the perceived height of the buildings in a sympathetic response to the surroundings.

ADDRESS Springfield Terrace, Upper Woodstock
ASSOCIATE ARCHITECT Architects Associated
CLIENT Headstart Developments
STRUCTURAL ENGINEER Gary De Villiers Sheard
CONTRACT VALUE R7.02 million
SIZE 133 units of 26 –73 square metres
GETTING THERE train to Woodstock ACCESS open

Uytenbogaardt & Rozendal Architects and Urban Designers 1993

Uytenbogaardt & Rozendal Architects and Urban Designers 1993

Old Castle Brewery

This conversion has resurrected a redundant turn-of-the-century building (originally a brewery, then a coldstore and warehouse) into a hive of artistic activity. Cavernous spaces, once bricked up, derelict and unoccupied, now provide studios for artists, sculptors and creative businesses.

Built in 1902 for the Castle Beer company, the building takes the form of a medieval castle complete with stone rusticated base, point arch openings and turreted top. Its impressive façade faces on to the railway line, with terraced levels rising from single storey to two, three and four storeys in the middle. Construction is a combination of load-bearing structural steel beams with massive riveted columns whose high load is graphically expressed by gargantuan stepped bases in the lower basement levels.

The 'restoration' embraces the building's multi-faceted history: plaster has been painstakingly removed to expose the original brick; old fridge doors, catwalks and aluminium ceilings from its incarnation as a coldstore have been retained. While new doors and windows do not replicate the existing ones, they are similarly proportioned. Floor finishes are mostly of tinted cement, while the walls are skimmed with cretestone in some areas. Mezzanine levels have been added to maximise usable floor area and additions such as toilets and stairs have been discreetly executed so as to minimise their impact on the building's original fabric. Each space has been overlaid with the signature of its tenant; the most interesting spaces include those of Headware Industries, Locomotive Media, André Carl Clothing, artist Lisa Brice and sculptor David Brown.

ADDRESS 6 Beach Road, Woodstock
SIZE 8000 square metres approximately
GETTING THERE train to Woodstock station
ACCESS announce yourself

Cape Town suburbs

Otten & Louw Architects 1985

Otten & Louw Architects 1985

Twin Houses, Observatory

These two compact houses are set in Observatory ('Obz'), a lively studenty eastern suburb of Cape Town. Characterised by its mix of residential (predominantly single-storey Victorian houses), commercial and industrial buildings, this is an area where gentrification rubs shoulders with gentle decay.

Externally, the most striking features are the large corrugated iron roofs that shelter the houses, drawing in light and framing views through clerestory windows. These are visually dominant during the day but at night they float weightlessly as light from inside glows through the glass panels between their supporting joists.

The neighbourhood's mishmash of walls and gates sets the cue for a fragmented boundary providing a foil to the large expanse of roof. A play is made of the different wall elements – a tall masonry wall securing privacy for the herb garden off the kitchen is followed by a low infill panel set back to form the gate. Differentiated only by their method of construction, two walls of equal height and colour complete the composition (the first is masonry, the last an infill panel).

On entering, you are drawn into the house as the roof sweeps up from a height of 2.1 metres at the entrance to create the double-storey volume of the 'public' living area – a buffer zone between the parents' domain on the mezzanine level above and the children's bedrooms and study/playroom in the front of the house. Here, a break in the roof suggests a disengagement which recalls the notion of the covered *stoep*. Internally, there is a minimal approach to the definition of spaces: the kitchen and dining area are kept open-plan; varying colour gradations in floor materials are used to demarcate various spaces; rooflights and the low drop of the roof are used to highlight entrances and punctuate transition areas. The result is a light, spacious quality that belies the tightness of the space.

Bert Pepler 1994

Cape Town suburbs

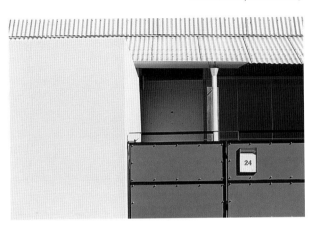

Cape Town suburbs

Bert Pepler 1994

Walls are generally kept bare and white, or panelled with plywood sepeli with aluminium trim, lending a warmth to the spaces while at the same time concealing cupboards. The back walls are finished in a different material to the rest of the house, thus making a visual reference to the juxtaposition of textures – peeling paint, spray paint, adjustments to old houses – which typifies this part of Cape Town. These consequently read as holding walls into which each new house appears to slot.

The interplay between inside and outside spaces is intrinsic to the design of these two houses. Their L-shape plans wrap around an internal courtyard which is visible from every room and which acts as a focus point, an extension of the glazed living-room spaces. A sense both of complete privacy and total openness has been achieved – from the street, the only indication of the plan arrangement of these two houses is a tell-tale palm tree peeking through between the rooftops.

Meticulously detailed throughout, these houses demonstrate an intelligent response to the surrounding architecture without reproducing its forms.

ADDRESS 24 and 24a Nuttall Road, Observatory
CLIENT I S Swanepoel
STRUCTURAL ENGINEER Henry Fagan & Partners
SIZE 300 square metres (total), 150 square metres (each house)
GETTING THERE train to Observatory station. From Lower Main Road walk down Trill Road and take the first turning on your right into Nuttall Road
ACCESS none

Cape Town suburbs

Bert Pepler 1994

Bert Pepler 1994

Hartleyvale Hockey Stadium

In early 1995, Cape Town accepted the invitation to host the qualifying tournament of the 1996 Atlanta Olympic Games women's hockey. This complex, which comprises a synthetic hockey pitch and a 2000-seater stadium accommodating offices, reception and changing rooms, was designed and constructed at a break-neck speed of less than ten months to be ready for the tournament in October 1995.

The project constituted the upgrading of an existing derelict sports ground and, despite a very tight budget, it included extensive landscaping which improved the local environment in the process. Seen as one of the early steps in Cape Town's (ultimately unsuccessful) bid to host the 2004 Olympic Games, its holistic approach has set an encouraging precedent for other would-be Olympic venues, gaining a unanimous thumbs-up from professionals and public alike.

The stadium stands in a parkland setting close to the residential area of Observatory. Framed on either side by slender, cigar-shaped lighting masts, it is set against the stunning backdrop of Table Mountain. The stand is a lightweight articulated structure, its appeal lying in the transparency of its construction: all the materials are revealed and clearly legible. The expressive character of the modular, tensile fabric roof is at once a visual delight and structurally economic. The floating canopy and seating mound form one of the building's two structurally independent elements; the first-floor offices and reception rooms nestled below form the other.

The principal structure consists of eight main columns, each supporting two concrete 'raker' and seating beams as well as a bay of the roof structure. This comprises three projecting steel booms of which adjacent pairs from adjoining bays are connected to create a continuous spine. The booms have spreaders and three tension rods spread radially around

Cape Town suburbs

GAPP Architects & Urban Designers 1995

GAPP Architects & Urban Designers 1995

them (to prevent buckling), allowing very light members to be used. The tension fabric roof is the largest of its kind in South Africa to date. Steel cables tie outwards on to the light masts to provide additional stability. The off-shutter members are carefully sculpted to reflect their structural purpose and left exposed internally, saving the cost of finishes. The main façade is supported by a series of vertical trusses.

When in use, the stadium acts as a festival tent; when vacant, it is an evocative and ethereal set piece.

Cape Town suburbs

ADDRESS Liesbeek Parkway, Observatory
ASSOCIATE ARCHITECT ACG Architects
CLIENT Cape Town City Council
STRUCTURAL ENGINEER Henry Fagan & Partners
CONTRACT VALUE R18 million
GETTING THERE train to Observatory station
ACCESS either by appointment through Mr Peters on 021 448 8653 between 7.00–16.15 weekdays, or just announce yourself to the caretaker on duty during stadium opening hours (7.00–19.00 every day)

GAPP Architects & Urban Designers 1995

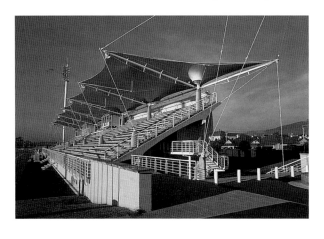

Cape Town suburbs

GAPP Architects & Urban Designers 1995

The Baxter Theatre

This is architect Jack Barnett's finest work and one of Cape Town's most interesting buildings. Located just below the University of Cape Town's College of Music (also by Barnett), it forms part of a complex which includes a concert hall and glazed foyer.

From the main road the solid brick masses of theatre and concert hall have distinctly different characters and forms: the theatre reads as a compact vertical brick pile topped with a tightly fitting roof; by contrast, the concert hall is planar, convoluted and airy, sheltered by a cantilevered metal roof which binds the whole and extends over the curved entrance ramp. Like a vast upside-down egg-tray, its underside is dimpled by clusters of brightly coloured fibreglass downlights. In 1970s-style orange, these look somewhat garish during the day but when lit at night make the roof appear completely weightless and give a fantastic glow to the building. Externally the choice of materials is limited to aluminium and glass or roughly chopped brick for walls, slate for floors, and corten steel (a special alloy which develops a protective rust coating) for the roofing.

The most exciting internal space is the theatre foyer which appears as a voluminous enclosure of the sloping site. With its cascading terraces, each linked to an external courtyard, it forms a continuation of the surrounding gardens. The use of corbels, piers, stepped walling and brick screens exploits the decorative qualities of brick to the maximum, adding a rugged richness to the space.

Intimately scaled and baroque-inspired, the theatre has a contemporary character, rich in colour and design. Additional accommodation includes dressing rooms, cast and orchestra lounges, a small rehearsal room and a self-contained TV-studio complex which serves the university as a whole.

The most distinctive features of the concert hall are its generous

Jack Barnett & Leslie Broer 1977

Jack Barnett & Leslie Broer 1977

proportions, circular plan and the unusual structure of its roof (which has 20 precast concrete girders on its underside, tied in a central core supported by columns at their perimeter). The combination of open trusses and concealed lighting produces decorative shadow effects across the ceiling, giving the structure lightness. Seating is arranged asymmetrically so that the audience is aware of itself, creating a dynamic relationship between performers and viewers.

As a university building, the Baxter Theatre accommodates a broad range of academic and social functions, ranging from conferences and lectures to graduation ceremonies. It is also a social centre for the lower campus – the self-service restaurant caters for students during the day and theatre-goers decked out for performances during the evening.

Cape Town suburbs

ADDRESS Main Road, Rondebosch
CLIENT University of Cape Town
STRUCTURAL ENGINEER Liebenberg & Stander
ACCESS open Monday to Saturday 8.00–22.30, Sunday 8.00–18.00

Jack Barnett & Leslie Broer 1977

Jack Barnett & Leslie Broer 1977

University of Cape Town Education Building

The nucleus of the University of Cape Town's middle campus, this building was designed as the link between the new development and the upper campus (the original university) from which it is severed by the M3 motorway.

Designing new faculty blocks to harmonise with old is always difficult. Architects confronted by this challenge invariably fall into two camps: those choosing to put their own stamp on the site with an injection of modern architecture; and those working slavishly to blend in with the existing traditional buildings. Here, Uytenbogaardt & Rozendal had already set a precedent for new, modern architecture with their sports centre (located directly opposite, across the motorway). This used the black tarmac of the road below the university residences, widened by a black tile façade, as a cut-off perimeter to allow stylistic freedom on the main campus. The middle campus planners could have extended this notion, using the intervention of the motorway to justify a change of style. Instead, however, they chose to compromise.

Aesthetically, the result is a hotchpotch which seeks unification with the original university through the choice of materials, while at the same time harking back to early European models for a sense of grandeur. A hipped, clay-tiled roof, buff brick walls and relentless, modular office windows characterise the basic box form of the building. Overlaid on to this is an environmental armature formed by yellow brick tower-like elements (apparently inspired by the dreaming spires of Oxford University) and a plastered screen (an attempt to overlay some of the proportions of the older buildings).

At ground level the building incorporates two major pedestrian routes which run from the historic Rustenberg Summer House (built in 1760

Elliott Grobelaar Revel Fox & Partners 1986

Elliott Grobelaar Revel Fox & Partners 1986

and located just below the motorway), reflecting the way in which the geometry of the old campus has been applied to the new development. One of these routes forms a diagonal link to the summerhouse; the other passes through arcades and colonnades on the formal north and west elevations.

The building houses the faculties of education and adult education, the department of extramural studies and the Professional Communication Unit, together with student and institutional services, conference facilities, a small cafeteria and a restaurant. The majority of this accommodation is organised around a large internal quad which forms the social focus of the building. The remainder (approximately one third of its area) is planned in semi-underground or ground-level structures with terraced roofscapes.

Despite the fact that the building is packed to the gills with different activities, its layout is lucid even to a visitor. Circulation areas are uncluttered, generous and light-filled. Some of the exterior detailing is successfully carried through internally and is extended to the design of the adjacent student housing development.

Cape Town suburbs

ADDRESS Middle Campus, University of Cape Town, Rondebosch
CLIENT University of Cape Town
STRUCTURAL ENGINEER Liebenberg & Stander
SIZE 14,000 square metres gross (9000 square metres assignable)
GETTING THERE from Cape Town via De Waal Drive and Rhodes Drive
ACCESS announce yourself

Elliott Grobelaar Revel Fox & Partners 1986

Elliott Grobelaar Revel Fox & Partners 1986

Sports Science Institute

Aimed at harnessing sporting talent, the Sports Science Institute is the first of its kind in South Africa. The building's two brick-clad blocks are articulated to reflect their different qualities and functions: the semi-public auditorium, swimming pool, gymnasium and running track are housed in the two-storey south block, a clerestoried shed-like structure providing the required natural light, large spans and open planning; the six-storey north block contains services, cellular offices and research and teaching spaces with parking at ground level. A double-volume galleria with a half-barrel-vaulted skylight acts as the link between the blocks and as a foyer to the auditorium. This long, light-filled entrance space sets the tone for the atmosphere of cool efficiency which typifies the whole.

The north block's first and second floors consist of galleried research laboratories and a range of consulting rooms set around a large multipurpose exercise hall – the focus of their activities. Extending from this, an external elevated track allows athletes to run into the building so that their movements can be electronically measured on force plates incorporated in the track floor. Among the sports bodies occupying the upper levels is the South African Rugby Football Union, whose offices contain a prominent photograph of Nelson Mandela in Springbok cap and shirt – an image that brings home the importance of sport in South Africa.

ADDRESS 1 Boundary Road, Newlands
CLIENTS Sports Science Institute of South Africa/University of Cape Town
STRUCTURAL ENGINEER Liebenberg & Stander
CONTRACT VALUE R25 million
SIZE 11,000 square metres
GETTING THERE train to Newlands station
ACCESS by appointment (contact M Higgins on 021 686 6968)

MLH Architects & Planners 1995

MLH Architects & Planners 1995

Ohlsson's Breweries silo

A large, ungainly industrial building in the middle of an upmarket residential area, this grain silo aspires quite simply to go unnoticed. The building comprises 12 bins, each with a capacity of 970 cubic metres, arranged in a cruciform rather than the usual rectangular plan so as to mitigate the visual impact of their bulk. Height has been limited to match that of the site's tallest existing building. As a result, the silo's lower portion, the underbin area, is buried approximately 4 metres below ground level.

The concrete silo is clad in a brick skin which gives a sense of scale and articulation to an otherwise featureless structure. A pitched roof, reminiscent of Cape Town's older industrial buildings, floats above a band of glazing which allows light into the overbin area. The appearance of the building also responds to the aesthetic tradition of the older buildings, such as the oast houses on the site.

The project is part of an upgrading of Ohlsson's Cape Breweries which has also included the renovation of the lager brewing building and a new elevated walkway which threads in and around the site – through the bottling hall, over the cellars and truck loading bays – to link up with the new visitors' centre (see page 92).

(see page 92)

ADDRESS corner Boundary and Main Roads, Newlands
CLIENT South African Breweries Ltd
STRUCTURAL ENGINEER Ove Arup Inc.
CONTRACT VALUE R5 million
SIZE 300 square metres
GETTING THERE train to Newlands station
ACCESS none

Cape Town suburbs

MLH Architects & Planners 1994

MLH Architects & Planners 1994

SAB Visitors Centre

Engulfed by the waft of malt on arrival at this centre, you are left in no doubt that you are at the heart of beer production (South African Breweries operates a large unit in the area, see page 90). The site's association with beer production dates back to the nineteenth century when two Cape Town businessmen, Jacob Letterstedt and Anders Ohlsson, developed a successful beer trade here. The business, Ohlsson's Cape Breweries, merged with South African Breweries in 1956.

To reconstruct the history of beer making in the Cape, the scheme entailed the restoration of two existing buildings, the old Mariendahl Brewery (built in 1859 by Letterstedt) and the malthouse kiln (built by Ohlsson 33 years later). The brief also called for the provision of lecture, dining and pub facilities for staff, a souvenir shop and the re-use of the 1863 distillery as an environmental centre.

In handling the building's new programme, the architect (who was also involved in the restoration of Cape Town's old castle) chose to complement by contrast – no attempt is made to blend the new fabric with the old. The integrity of the new project lies instead in its differentiation through the choice of materials and a colour coding device that loudly announces its newness. Used for handrails and fittings, this coding device connects the various new structures and choreographs your journey through the centre, leading you through the sequential steps of beer-making.

The transparency of glass is a key motif: it is used for junctions between structures, highlighting the separation between old and new; a glass pyramid at the main entrance rises from pavement level to bring light to the original ground level below; a glass lift acts as the predominant link between all levels; a cranked glass-covered path has a water feature by Durban sculptor Etienne de Kock (symbolising the importance of the

Gabriel Fagan Architects 1995

Gabriel Fagan Architects 1995

Newlands Spring water to the quality of the beer) extending along its length. This leads to an archaeological site of early malting works.

The car park, ordinarily the most unimaginatively designed amenity, is here an unusual and elegant feature in its own right. A post-tensioned flat slab with mushroom columns allows for a beam-free lower level dotted with shallow recessed light fittings. Puncturing the slab, large circular openings pour natural light into the lower parking level and allow poplar trees to grow through, providing shade for the cars parked above. The slab slopes a metre from end to end while its column structure follows the curve of the adjacent main road to create a dynamic near-natural situation enhanced by the planted grading of the site around the lower level. Accommodating 200 bays split equally over its two levels, the car park fits unobtrusively into its surroundings.

Cape Town suburbs

ADDRESS Ohlsson's Brewery, 3 Main Road, Newlands
CLIENT South African Breweries
STRUCTURAL ENGINEER Henry Fagan & Partners
GETTING THERE train to Newlands station
ACCESS open

Gabriel Fagan Architects 1995

Gabriel Fagan Architects 1995

Vineyard Road Gallery

This project was born of an exceptional client/architect collaboration. Started over a decade ago, it is scheduled to reach painstaking completion by the client (who is also acting as contractor) in 1998.

The design brief had three essential requirements: to provide new premises for an established antiques business; to develop an exhibition space which could be used either independently or to support the gallery's activities; and to provide a director's suite which would act as the fulcrum for both enterprises. The unfinished work already has a powerful and intriguing presence. A subtle solution to an awkwardly shaped site, it presents a visually complex form and offers endless vistas for discovery.

The design is both tempered and enriched by its location between commercial and residential areas. A layered façade buffers its impact on the neighbouring houses while its gradually escalating mass is contained in an abrupt wall at its commercial edge. The varying responses are bound by the street façade in a continuous, undulating threshold which draws one into the building's volume. The entrance is to be celebrated in travertine, granite and steel. Through to the rear, the gallery is a light-filled volume with an ambiguity designed to allow exhibitors freedom to inhabit the space as they wish.

ADDRESS 37 Vineyard Road, Claremont
CLIENT Hans Niehaus
STRUCTURAL ENGINEER Hickson-Mahony & Meny-Gibert
CONTRACT VALUE R2 million SIZE 500 square metres
GETTING THERE take the M3 towards Muizenberg. After approximately 10 kilometres take the Claremont turning. At the traffic lights approaching the town centre on Protea Road, the gallery can be seen on your right behind the big blue gum tree ACCESS open

Cape Town suburbs

Norbert Rozendal 1984–98

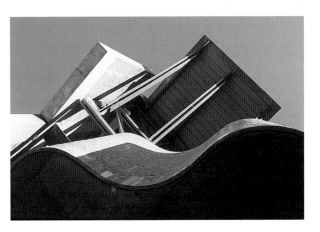

Cape Town suburbs

Norbert Rozendal 1984–98

University of the Western Cape Library

Cape Town suburbs

This library binds a varied group of major buildings around the open space which acts as the university's gravitational centre. Its triangular plan completes the fanning central space and provides access to it via gateways at each corner.

The main approach to the campus leads to the back of the library. A stepped concourse draws you into the quad. Splaying to one side, the library's façade is articulated by a zigzagging colonnade which weaves it into the public space. The full-height glazing of the façade is interrupted by a curved wall marking the library entrance and by brick piers which continue to support the roof.

Internal organisation generates from a central helical ramp which was specially developed to provide the spatial fluidity needed to accommodate expansion or shrinkage in the book collection while maintaining sequential continuity. Rising to large modules of split-level library space, the ramp system creates an armature of space around a glazed atrium, bringing light and air into the centre of this large building. Particular attention is given to the design of a variety of reading environments. Banded facebrick is the predominant finish inside and out.

ADDRESS West Campus, University of the Western Cape, Bellville
ASSOCIATE ARCHITECT Julian Elliot
CLIENT University of the Western Cape
STRUCTURAL ENGINEER Naylor Naylor & Theron
SIZE 12,500 square metres
GETTING THERE from Cape Town take the N2 motorway to Modderdam Road
ACCESS open

Munnik Visser Black Fish & Partners 1988

Cape Town suburbs

Munnik Visser Black Fish & Partners 1988

Cape Flats

Marconi Beam Housing Project

Part of a mixed-use development, the Marconi Beam housing project was built with the aim of creating higher density housing for the urban poor living in the shacks nearby. The settlement had been in the spotlight for years: at one point, the squatters living there were threatened with forcible removal, but finally an agreement was reached allocating them one quarter of the 240-hectare site for affordable formal housing.

This scheme is distinguished from others by the way it embraces ideas of economic sustainability and community development: the community has been provided with commercial properties (which it can trade on the market or use for its own business needs) as well as community facilities, schools, clinics and so on, owned by a community trust.

Innovation is to be found in the planning rather than the architecture. The dwellings stay within the limitations of subsidised housing, ranging from variously sized groupings of rectangular rooms to single-room 'starter' units on to which additions can be made. Collectively, these are intended as the building blocks for a varied urban landscape. The reality, however, is an all-too-familiar monotonous sprawl.

ADDRESS Joe Slovo Park, Freedom Way, Milnerton
PROJECT CO-ORDINATOR Alastair Rendall
CLIENT Marconi Beam Informal Settlement
COST PER UNIT R17,500–R65,000 (including land)
SIZE 13.4–71.7 square metres per unit
GETTING THERE take the Milnerton off-ramp from the N1 highway north. Proceed north on Koeberg Road for approximately 4 kilometres and take a right turn into Freedom Way (immediately before the tall block of flats to your left). Proceed for approximately half a kilometre
ACCESS open

Cape Flats

DAG (Development Action Group) 1996

Cape Flats

DAG (Development Action Group) 1996

Ulwazi Youth Centre

The Ulwazi Youth Centre is in Langa, one of the oldest black townships of the Western Cape, 10 kilometres from the centre of Cape Town. Historically, the area has been torn apart by political conflict and violence, gaining notoriety for its 1989 youth gang killings. In the absence of any public facilities other than 'shebeens' (illegal bars), the centre was set up to provide alternative programmes to get young people off the streets.

Considerable groundwork preceded any architectural proposals. Over a two-year period, an ambitious brief was defined by representatives from the various gangs and youth organisations. Proposals were prepared and funds raised to build the first phase of Ulwazi in 1991 (a second phase has been planned but has not been completed). The building comprises three rectangular elements – a large hall and two double-storey structures housing classrooms and office space. Contained by chainlink fencing, an external area provides additional classrooms and a protected play space. The design is based around a strong circulation route, loosely linking the sections and enclosing a courtyard for games. All spaces are multifunctional, with strong forms, bright colours and varied finishes.

ADDRESS 36 Njoli Street, Langa
CLIENT Ulwazi Youth Centre
STRUCTURAL ENGINEER Karl Hvidsten Structural Engineers
CONTRACT VALUE R1.05 million SIZE 780 square metres
GETTING THERE enter Langa at the first entrance from Cape Town on the N2 highway. Drive along Bhunga Avenue (palm trees on the left) until a four-way intersection; turn right into Washington Street and proceed for approximately 3 kilometres. Pass the old beer hall on the right, then turn right into Njoli Street. The building is at the end of the street
ACCESS open

Cape Flats

CS Studio Architects 1989–96

CS Studio Architects 1989–96

Mzamomhle Clinic

Situated in Browns Farm, a dismal township on the Cape Flats, this clinic was financed and facilitated by the Independent Development Trust, a non-governmental organisation. The project was begun in 1993, the explosive year before the elections. An enormous amount of consultation was needed to gain not only the co-operation of the intransigent old local authorities but also the trust of the communities themselves, who subsequently became actively involved in the project's progress.

Influenced by climate, environment, custom and a very tight budget, the design creates a simple order in the surrounding urban confusion by forming definite edges and positive communal spaces. Its roughly L-shaped form is orientated to shield the entrance court from summer winds and catch the sun in winter. On the north the roof extends to provide shelter for outdoor waiting areas and for the service bay which once a month accommodates a mobile X-ray truck. Treatment rooms are separated from public areas so that the main waiting rooms and toilets can also be used for after-hours community activities. The colours – bright yellow, acid green, white, blue – reflect the vibrant and jarring nature of township structures.

ADDRESS Mzamomhle, Browns Farm, Philippi
CLIENT Browns Farm Clinic Committee
STRUCTURAL ENGINEER Ove Arup Inc.
CONTRACT VALUE R750,000 SIZE 550 square metres
GETTING THERE from the N2 east from Cape Town, take the M7 exit south towards Mitchells Plain and then to the left the M9 East Lansdowne Road into Philippi Industria. Take the third turning on the right towards Philippi Station and then the first left after crossing Sheffield Street. The building is to the left of two facebrick schools
ACCESS open

Cape Flats

Gideon Scott Architect 1995

Transportable post boxes

If you never venture beyond the urban and developed residential parts of South Africa, you are unlikely to catch sight of these delightful, fantastically functional post boxes, which are installed only in developing and underdeveloped areas such as townships, informal settlements and rural areas. In these areas, where 'spaza' shops (informal shops) have long since used freight containers as a cost-effective alternative to formal buildings, the bright red, container-like collection points appear entirely in keeping.

The steel boxes provide postal addresses for the local people. They measure 6 x 2.5 metres and, weighing a whopping 6.5 tonnes, sit on a concrete slab. Intelligent features include solar panels for lighting at night supported by a mast to one side; flip-up canopies providing protection from the elements; and a perforated slot above the boxes to allow for ventilation, keeping the containers cool. There are two types – with either 800 or 400 lockable boxes – also containing a small office for postal collection and delivery.

With R190 million of the Post Office budget for the 1995/96 financial year set aside for its Reconstruction and Development Programme, the company is clearly 'putting its money where its mouth is'. The millionth address box at a transportable mail collection point (approximately a sixth of the addresses to which post is delivered in the whole country) was celebrated in April 1996. There are plans to install at least a further four million addresses.

Cape Flats

ADDRESS in townships, informal settlements and some rural areas
CLIENT South African Postal Service
COST PER UNIT R54,000
SIZE 2.5 x 6 x 2.64 metres

South African Postal Services 1993

Cape Flats

South African Postal Services 1993

Nyanga Junction retail centre

Strategically located at an important transport node on the Cape Flats, this retail development marks a pioneering venture initiated by local black entrepreneurs – a hitherto marginalised sector of the business community. Tenants range from national retailers to small local traders.

The site is a narrow strip of land which once belonged to the railways and which formed part of a buffer zone separating the black communities to the east and the coloured communities to the west. Its strong north–south axis, the existing railway bridge and the level of the station platform were the key design determinants. The result is a 390-metre linear building characterised by a tough industrial aesthetic. Although it is the largest structure for miles around, it is neither overscaled nor alienating. Clever articulation, transparency and deep setbacks take the sting out of its scale and its raw functional materials.

The length of the building is differentiated into three distinct sections, with a double-storey market hall contained by single-storey approaches. Visually the sections are unified by a barrel-vaulted roof structure and the rhythm of robust structural steelwork. Throughout there is an animated street-like bustle.

ADDRESS facing intersection of Downs and Duinefontein Roads, Nyanga
CLIENTS Combi & Co (developer), Montsi & Associates (project preparation and co-ordination)
STRUCTURAL ENGINEER Sonnekus & Toerien
CONTRACT VALUE R30 million
GETTING THERE from the N2 east from Cape Town take the M10 Duinefontein exit south, cross over the M18 Klipfontein and the building is about 1 kilometre on the left
ACCESS open

Cape Flats

GAPP Architects & Urban Designers 1995

Cape Flats

GAPP Architects & Urban Designers 1995

Uthango Lotyebiselwano (Learning Circle)

Carin Smuts of CS Studio is one of the most relevant architects practising in South Africa today. Her work in the Cape's townships has consistently pushed back the boundaries of the architect's conventional role, involving an unprecedented level of engagement (see Ulwazi Youth Centre, page 104).

This project was initiated by the young people of the community after the 1976 riots. Driven by their frustration at the lack of alternatives to substandard government education, they wanted to focus not on violence but rather on the development of the community.

Working with Uthango, a community organisation promoting education, art and culture, CS Studio held many meetings and workshops to plan the building. The brief required an educational resource centre, overnight accommodation with a canteen, an arts centre and multipurpose cultural centre with a performance hall divided into three phases, of which the 'Learning Circle' is the first.

Situated in Nyanga, which is made up of formal housing, hostels and shacks, the building provides an exciting blend of indoor and outdoor spaces, consisting of a series of simple volumes and a pavilion around a courtyard amphitheatre.

The walkways, stairs and bridge bind the volumes together and add a dynamic quality to the space. A cranked wall with a splayed timber structure carrying the over-sailing roof through the existing trees marks the entrance to the building.

The brightly painted finishes and the robust timberwork are appropriate in the context; the timberwork in particular is of a high quality considering that workers received only nine weeks of carpentry training before starting work.

Cape Flats

CS Studio Architects 1989–96

Cape Flats

CS Studio Architects 1989–96

Unfortunately, following an unexplained dispute at the centre, the building was completely vandalised. At the time this guide was being written, it lay unused.

ADDRESS erf (plot) no. 1931 Thamsanga Street, Nyanga East
CLIENT Uthango Lotyebiselwano Association
STRUCTURAL ENGINEER Ninham Shand
CONTRACT VALUE R950,000
SIZE 789 square metres
GETTING THERE from the N2 take the Guguletu off-ramp into Duinefontein Road and drive until M9 Lansdowne Road. Turn left, then take the third turning to the left into Emmbry Street, then the first right into Second Street. Proceed and take the sixth road to the left into Thamsanga Street. The building is the second one on the right-hand side
ACCESS open

Cape Flats

CS Studio Architects 1989–96

CS Studio Architects 1989–96

Guguletu Multisport Complex

This complex was commissioned by the National Sports Congress as the first of a proposed series of indoor sports facilities to be built in the township areas.

Set in a large, desolate field surrounded by mainly single-storey houses, the complex comprises a multi-use sports hall plus changing rooms, washrooms, committee rooms, meeting areas and space for general social use. Committee and changing rooms are cleverly arranged to capitalise on natural light from the translucent roof above the main foyer. Ancillary accommodation is wrapped around the hall, reducing the overall scale of the building and articulating its façades. Seating tiers along the length of the hall are expressed externally as corrugations on the side walls, providing deep shadowed recesses which lift the apparent weight of the building. The large barrel-vaulted hall is fully exposed on the north elevation, creating a sense of civic presence in the sprawling urban landscape.

ADDRESS corner NY1 and NY2, Guguletu
ASSOCIATE ARCHITECT Meirelles Lawson Architects
CLIENT Facilities Committee of the National Sports Congress
STRUCTURAL ENGINEER De Villiers Hulme
CONTRACT VALUE R1.3 million
SIZE 1,050 square metres
GETTING THERE take the Guguletu turn-off from the N2 highway and travel south on Duinefontein Road. Turn left at Klipfontein Road (major intersection). Go over the railway; turn right into NY1 at the first set of traffic lights and drive for about 1 kilometre. The centre is on your left
ACCESS open

Cape Flats

Jo Noero Architects 1994

Jo Noero Architects 1994

New Crossroads Community Centre

'All warmer climates require of architecture is to breathe; the *werf* verandah yard, threshold between shelter and exposure – a shared place of work/encounter/social life – is for me the quintessential African space. Like the heart in the middle of the body as the centre of human emotion, architecture here should not belong to eastern or western paradigms – it is feeling first, and thought second.'

These views, expressed by Etienne Rousseau Bruwer, are reflected in his design for this community centre. Based on the idea of a covered kraal, it is a four-stage development consisting of a central hall in an open court encircled by a doughnut ring of amenities.

To date, only the hall and basic perimeter wall have been built. The elements nonetheless give a flavour of the whole. A gothic arch provides the section for a lightweight aluminium structure containing the simple volume of the hall. The wall by contrast is a heavy mass of free-flowing forms, seemingly moulded from the very earth of the site.

ADDRESS Corner of Koornhof and Nontulo Streets, New Crossroads, Nyanga
CLIENT Ikapa Town Council & New-Cross Civic Association
STRUCTURAL ENGINEER Hemingway Isaacs Coetzee and Jeffares Green Group CONTRACT VALUE R1 million (first phase)
SIZE 500 square metres (hall and offices)
GETTING THERE take the Guguletu turn-off from the N1 highway and travel south on Duinefontein Road. Turn left at Klipfontein Road (major intersection). Go over the railway and turn left into NY1 at the first set of traffic lights. Off NY1 turn left into NY3. The centre is on your right at the first junction as NY3 becomes Koornhof Road
ACCESS open

Cape Flats

Etienne Rousseau Bruwer Architects 1993

Etienne Rousseau Bruwer Architects 1993

Cape Flats

Mzamomtshaba Primary School

The programme for this school called for the construction of an open-air forum area (to be roofed in phase two), a library, an administration block, computer and science facilities. The second block of classrooms will be phased in when the surrounding settlement grows in size.

The school is located in Driftsands, an informal settlement on the periphery of Cape Town formed during the period of political unrest in the 1980s, when people were forced to flee from other areas. The settlement has only recently received electricity, and there are few opportunities or facilities here. Consequently, the school has to fulfil several functions – as a community centre, a centre for adult education, a focus for cultural activities and a link to the outside world.

In order to facilitate such varied uses, the building consists of two distinct units. The first, based around the forum area, is intended to act as a civic centre for the town. It has a more sophisticated level of architecture than the other unit and is located closer to the entrance to the complex.

The second zone is the children's classroom block. Here the language is more playful, the scale and massing of the buildings more intimate. The buildings respond to the nature of the dwellings around them by using similar massing and materials.

ADDRESS Driftsands
CLIENT Department of Works
CONTRACT VALUE R4.5 million SIZE 1,300 square metres
GETTING THERE take N1 towards Somerset West. Turn left at exit 25 (Blue Downs/Khayalitsha) then left at the T-junction. Take the first turning to the right into Driftsands and proceed to the end of the cul-de-sac
ACCESS open

Cape Flats

Stefan Antoni Architects 1998

Stefan Antoni Architects 1998

Cape Town, surrounding areas

House Albertyn

A colourful, dynamic collision of forms, this 'folly' seems at first sight a radically incongruous addition to its suburban setting. Set 2 metres above street level against the slopes of Paarl Mountain, its modest site is a sub-division of the garden of an existing 1920s house.

The main approach consists of a steel bridge over an existing swimming pool in the centre of the site. Clearly visible from the street, the main living area and focus of the house is a double-volume glass box which opens on to the pool via a segmented glass 'garage' door.

The transparency of the living area contrasts with the insular, hearth-like service areas whose bulky forms echo the granite bulges on top of Paarl Mountain. Between the more solid kitchen and the glass cubicle is the jagged edge of a 'broken concrete slab' which sets the tone for a connection of skewed elements – nothing seems parallel or perpendicular.

Accommodated off the main living area at higher level are a smaller family room and two children's bedrooms playfully separated by a snaking wall which extends into the garden beyond. Overlooking both family areas, a bridge-like landing on the uppermost level provides a quiet study area and access to the secluded main bedroom.

ADDRESS 12 Timberon Street, Paarl
CLIENT Elzet and Christof Albertyn
STRUCTURAL ENGINEER Nortje & De Villiers
CONTRACT VALUE R600,000 SIZE 260 square metres
GETTING THERE from Central Cape Town take the highway N1 and continue along Paarl main road for about 5 kilometres until you reach the Protea Cinema (to your right). Turn left into Hout Street which is directly opposite; Timberon Street is the third turning on your left
ACCESS by appointment (telephone the architects on 021 872 6472)

Wessels Albertyn Architects 1995

Cape Town, surrounding areas

Wessels Albertyn Architects 1995

Dalweide Primary School

The plan of this primary school is generated by a triangular internal court defined by the building's three separate blocks – two double-storey classroom buildings form its main sides with administration offices closing its end. Bounded by walkways, the lively communal space is divided into two distinct parts by a central bridge-link connecting the school's junior and senior wings. The administration end is completely covered and, lit by rooflights, functions as an assembly hall. The narrower end is openair, with its circulation areas sheltered by exaggerated eaves.

Although the layout of the school is quite rational, its exterior gives the impression that riotous children had a hand in its assembly: downpipes are widely splaying, randomly cranked to meet jagged, projecting roof forms or partially encased in angular metal sleeves; red facebrick walls with variously sized windows are overlaid with irregular patches of brightly coloured plaster. But in fact there is very little about this design that is ad hoc: close inspection reveals precise detailing and the imaginative use of standard materials. Despite its barren surroundings, the school positively screams 'this is a fun place to be'.

ADDRESS Symphony Avenue, Paarl
CLIENT Die Areabestuurder, Wes-Kaap Onderswys-departement
STRUCTURAL ENGINEER R A Moffat
CONTRACT VALUE R4 million
SIZE 2,000 square metres
GETTING THERE from central Cape Town take N1 turn-off to Paarl (R45, Main Road); follow until the end and turn right into Lady Grey Street; at T-section turn left into Jan van Riebeeck Street; after 1.5 kilometres turn right into Bach Street. Take the first turning on your left into Symphony Avenue ACCESS announce yourself at reception

Wessels Albertyn Du Toit 1995

Wessels Albertyn Du Toit 1995

Central Johannesburg

Electric Workshop

On the west side of the CBD, the site of Johannesburg's first power station (built in 1905) is now the focus of an ambitious urban renewal programme aimed at turning its various buildings into cultural, educational, commercial and entertainment venues.

This workshop – the conversion of the old power-house machine hall into an exhibition space – is part of a planned science and technology centre. The initiative has been supported by the city authorities, who have funded the basic structure of display areas and circulation systems as well as fire-safety measures to bring the space up to modern standards.

The proposal, a steel and concrete insertion, continues the theme of a battery of freestanding machines on podiums running through each structural bay of the existing shed. The design spills through the space, incorporating or bypassing existing features such as columns to become a large, elaborate display case. Modern components are introduced to celebrate the engineering technology of the period without imitating or changing the integrity of the original structural components. The design recalls the bowed steel balconies and rolling stock undercarriages of the old tram cars, the system for which the power station was originally built.

The building provided one of the key sites for the Johannesburg Biennale, the country's first international art exhibition.

ADDRESS Electric Workshop, Newtown [43 B8]
CLIENT Greater Johannesburg Transitional Metropolitan Council
STRUCTURAL ENGINEER Kampel Abramowitz Yawitch & Partners
SIZE 5000 square metres
GETTING THERE bus 62 or 63 to Newtown
ACCESS open

Central Johannesburg

Albonico & Sack Architects and Urban Planners 1995–

Central Johannesburg

Albonico & Sack Architects and Urban Planners 1995–

Workers' Library & Museum

Migrant worker hostels have long been the most emotive and potent manifestation of the apartheid labour system, and in recent years many of them have been demolished. However, this unique example, formerly the Electricity Workers' Compound, has been spared, conserved as an historic monument and converted into a resource centre. Originally built in 1905, it once accommodated 312 municipal workers, segregating them by gender, race and class. Now it provides workers with workshop, conference and, significantly, library and education facilities – commodities denied them under the apartheid regime.

Externally, the hostel has been restored to its former state. Internally, its east wing, accommodating the library component, has undergone changes including the addition of a mezzanine level and essentials such as insulation, ventilation and electrical installations. Restored dormitories and wash areas form a small permanent exhibition illustrating the harsh conditions under which the migrant workers lived.

The architects did not treat the buildings as precious objects but rather as workaday artefacts. While recording an extraordinarily sordid past, this 'ordinary' building makes a remarkable contribution to an optimistic future.

ADDRESS corner Jeppe and Bezuidenhout Streets, Newtown [43 B8]
CLIENT Johannesburg City Council
STRUCTURAL ENGINEER Johannesburg City Council
CONTRACT VALUE R1.3 million
SIZE 900 square metres
GETTING THERE bus 62 or 63 to Jeppe Street
ACCESS open Monday to Saturday 9.00–17.00

Central Johannesburg

Lipman Paine Architects 1995

Central Johannesburg

Lipman Paine Architects 1995

South Africa Reserve Bank

Set on the CBD periphery between glossy corporate giants and derelict industrial buildings, this is a sophisticated building which takes seriously both its function and its place in the city. Its purpose is twofold: to serve as a money distribution centre for the Gauteng commercial banking system and as a front office for the money and capital market department. It also provides a second office for executives from the Reserve Bank's head office when they are on business in Johannesburg.

The brief called for a fortified structure that would project an image of prestige, permanence and strength. The architects' response avoids the archetypal cop-outs: there is no techno-megalith, no neo-colonial pastiche. These city favourites were clearly inappropriate models for a building which, conceived during a sensitive period of political transition, was to be the first significant public work of the emerging democracy. Instead, the architects have taken a fragmented approach, intended to fuse African and Western traditions. A loose composition of geometric structures is in turn ordered by an axial, vaulted arcade designed to recall the classical dignity of the Roman forum. Mixed metaphors? Perhaps, but any possible contradictions are transcended by the intelligent way in which the building responds to its surroundings while conforming to a complex and demanding brief.

The division between functions is explicit. The high-security cash depot (along with parking facilities, services and security rooms) occupies a partially buried podium, strung with a sloping, facebrick façade. This kinks to a 10-metre perimeter wall containing the complex of smaller structures above, each of which has an individual identity and distinct plan-form: the auditorium (which is a circle), head-office facilities (a trapezium), staircases (triangular), lifts (square), washrooms (semicircular) and administrative offices (rectangular).

Central Johannesburg

Meyer Pienaar Architects & Urban Designers 1996

Meyer Pienaar Architects & Urban Designers 1996

The elements borrow their materials as well as their scale from their surroundings: red brick, dark granite, black aluminium, polished steel with copper roofing. The result is a delightful jumble which echoes the surrounding roofscape and which is best appreciated when cruising past on the M1 motorway.

At the reception control point, stairs and lift provide access to the 'public floor' of the bank, a mezzanine level overlooking the major public areas and the money market on the first floor. Support facilities provide a sequential spatial experience along the central axis which, punctuated by bridges links, terminates in a two-storey atrium which brings light into the centre of the building. Full-height glazing provides natural light, with selected views connecting interiors to landscaped areas outside. Detailing throughout is meticulous, rich and, in places, absolutely exquisite.

The building was slated by critics who questioned the appropriateness of such opulence and grandeur in a society struggling with homelessness and poverty. The cost of the building is in fact comparable to that of many of the city's corporate buildings. The only extravagance is spatial, particularly the over-generosity of circulation areas (a requirement of the brief was to provide accommodation for the envisioned growth of the bank to the year 2050).

ADDRESS corner West and Pritchard Streets, Newtown [43 B8]
CLIENT South Africa Reserve Bank
STRUCTURAL ENGINEER BKS Inc.
CONTRACT VALUE R80 million SIZE 24,000 square metres
GETTING THERE bus 10, 22 or 23 to Stock Exchange Terminus and proceed to the end of Pritchard Street
ACCESS none

Central Johannesburg

Meyer Pienaar Architects & Urban Designers 1996

Meyer Pienaar Architects & Urban Designers 1996

11 Diagonal Street

Chicago-based architect Helmut Jahn's first foray on South African turf is this provocative statement on the city's skyline. Dubbed 'the Diamond', it is a multi-faceted, shiny edifice containing a five-storey entrance atrium, 18 office floors and a machine floor, plus two penthouses each with a two-storey atrium (all are slightly different in area because of the building's sloping façades). Seen from head-on, the wedge looks more like a rocket than a diamond – slenderly proportioned, symmetrical, tapering to a spire. Its reinforced concrete structure is cocooned in pin-striped blue and silver silicon glazing, providing a reflective backdrop for the eclectic mix of surrounding buildings which are dwarfed by Jahn's construction, its scale appearing as alien as its futuristic imagery. A landscaped court at its base seems to have been designed less as a sympathetic gesture to pedestrians than as a means of keeping them at bay.

The architect believes that a building must have an impact on its environment, and this one certainly does: the glare from 'the Diamond' has caused a hazard to motorists and has sent the cooling systems of adjacent buildings into over-drive to deal with the reflected heat (the adjacent Stock Exchange was so dazzled that there was talk of a lawsuit against owners Anglo American Properties).

ADDRESS 11 Diagonal Street [43 B8]
ASSOCIATE ARCHITECT Louis Karol Architects
CLIENT Anglo American Properties (AMPROS)
STRUCTURAL ENGINEER Ove Arup & Partners
CONTRACT VALUE R70 million
GETTING THERE bus 10, 22, 34 to Johannesburg Stock Exchange Terminus
ACCESS to the foyer space only

Murphy/Jahn 1983

Murphy/Jahn 1983

Ernst & Young House

The site of this commercial redevelopment edges Diagonal Street, the historical remnant of the old city boundary. Here, at the meeting point between first- and third-world economies, street hawkers and Muti (traditional medicine) shops rub shoulders with the Johannesburg Stock Exchange and its attendant financial giants.

Executed in collaboration with the National Monuments Council, the scheme responds sensitively to the dynamics of the surrounding area. The site accommodates a tower component with retail space at ground level incorporating 'Trader's Alley', an informal area of stalls linking Pritchard and President Streets. In order to retain this trading alley, the design of the office tower was limited to the easternmost half of the site, with the tower orientated east–west. The symmetrical design of the main west façade responds to the axis set by 11 Diagonal Street situated directly opposite (see page 138).

A more upmarket trading image has replaced the gritty chaos of old, yet the flavour remains – a mix of bustling street life and the smell of fruit, curry powder and incense.

ADDRESS 4 Pritchard Street [43 D8]
CLIENT JOHNNIC (Johannesburg Consolidated Investment for the Mines Pension Fund)
STRUCTURAL ENGINEER Ove Arup Inc.
CONTRACT VALUE R40 million
SIZE 22,100 square metres
GETTING THERE take bus 10, 22 or 34 to Johannesburg Stock Exchange Terminus
ACCESS Trader's Alley is open; Ernst & Young House by appointment (contact Mrs Val Brits on 011–498 1000)

Central Johannesburg

RFB Architects 1992

RFB Architects 1992

Kerk Street mosque

The form, ornamentation and construction techniques employed in the design of this mosque are inspired by the traditional disciplines of Islamic art and architecture. Mayet's is an unsentimental approach which bridges modernity and history, creating here a building that responds not only to its downtown site but also to a whole culture that was once threatened with extinction under the grand apartheid plan.

As you approach from the north, the mosque is revealed framed within the arches of the BankCity development (see page 146), its cubic mass, dome and minaret presenting an idiomatic silhouette. It is a powerful presence, undaunted by the scale of its surroundings.

While the external walls of the mosque align with the site boundary, the prayer hall's internal volume pivots against the city grid to orientate itself towards Mecca. The tension arising from these opposing orders is subtly expressed by a fracture in the building's northern entrance corner and the slight asymmetry of the balcony drawing out of its main façade. The main dome on the north side of the mosque further reinforces this directional axis and constitutes one of a number of traditional elements. Access to the mosque is via the lobby on the building's south-west corner or steps to the main entrance at the junction of Kerk and Sauer Streets. These lead up to the level of the main prayer hall which is raised on the *piano nobile* above street level.

The main prayer hall is a triple-volume galleried space articulated through a gridwork of arches on pillars and segmental arches over segmental vaults. The vaults are interrupted by the dome which is raised on a drum that filters light into the interior directly above the *mihrab* (preacher's niche). The character of the basement mosque is dramatically different: this is an ethereal, crypt-like space whose heavy brick columns mushroom into delicate fan-vaults. Throughout, ornamentation and

Central Johannesburg

Muhammad Mayet Architect 1996

Muhammad Mayet Architect 1996

detailing enhance a sense of history and sanctity, providing an ambience for meditation and prayer in the heart of the city. Here, as in the main prayer hall, the juxtaposition of intricate plasterwork and raw brick is breathtaking. The use of load-bearing brick rather than the prevailing technology of reinforced concrete is integral to the design: it gives the interiors an incredible coolness and is exploited decoratively in the masonry techniques.

With the help of computer-generated drawings, the art of *muqarnas* stalactite design was revived for the detailing of the spindly minaret balcony. Though thousands of years old, it is a technique which, because of its strong geometry, lends itself to CAD modelling. Designing in three dimensions, the architect was able to create beautifully proportioned internal spaces.

The mosque was built by a team of local workers who learned to make arches, domes and vaults by hand, using only stock bricks and mortar.

ADDRESS Kerk Street (corner of Sauer Street) [43 D8]
CLIENT Jumah Masgied Society
ASSOCIATE ARCHITECT Abdel Wahid El-Wakil
STRUCTURAL ENGINEER Jan Wesseloo
CONTRACT VALUE R6 million
SIZE 2200 square metres
GETTING THERE bus 10, 22 or 34 to Stock Exchange Terminus, or 67 or 79 to BankCity
ACCESS open (remove shoes at entrance; women must be appropriately dressed)

Central Johannesburg

Muhammad Mayet Architect 1996

Central Johannesburg

Muhammad Mayet Architect 1996

BankCity

Spanning four city blocks, with three more on the drawing board, BankCity is arguably the country's largest and most controversial project. Axially designed, the four grey, granite, monolithic neo-classical blocks house the headquarters of First National Bank, formerly Barclays SA. It is the work of Revel Fox, who has a reputation for clean, stark, modernist buildings (see CPA Headquarters, page 22, and BP Centre, page 34) and who is widely regarded as one of South Africa's foremost architects. Little wonder then that a collective cry of 'what happened?' went up from the profession, baffled by his retrogressive choice of expression.

I asked the architect whether he thought there was a contradiction between the architectural language and the brief, which I imagined sought a design for the twenty-first century:

RF Everybody thinks that, yes, but finance houses want to show that they've been there a long time and that they intend to be there a long time in the future, which doesn't necessarily mean that they have to have the trappings of the future or somebody's idea of what African architecture in the twenty-first century must be like – most of it is spurious nonsense.

It wasn't necessarily a forward-looking building at all, it's just a building. The language of neo-classicism is one that keeps popping up and will pop up in the twenty-first and twenty-second centuries in various forms so I don't have to tell you about the durability of the humanism aspect in neo-classicism, in terms of being a recurrent theme in architecture. Put another way, I didn't have an architecture to suggest for a seven-block central urban building other than the International Style which I was brought up in, which I didn't think was necessary or appropriate.

Revel Fox & Partners 1995

Central Johannesburg

Revel Fox & Partners 1995

So there we are, an inadequacy, if you like, a loss of courage, a loss of … not necessarily of courage. It took a lot more courage to start off as a golden idealist in the modern movement and then turn.

So was he responding to client pressure?

RF Oh no, I'm entirely to blame. I think I could have persuaded the bank in other directions. I accept full responsibility for the appearance of the building. There was no client pressure. The wish on my part was to give it a resolution that would satisfy everyone in the banking community and everyone that uses it. There's a hell of a lot of rubbish talked about the democratisation of architecture, mostly among a very élite modern group who build buildings which have absolutely no democratic content. But this building – despite the fact it has all the colonial overtones and all the élitism of the tradition – has a wider acceptance than any other contemporary building in Johannesburg.

ADDRESS four city blocks bisected by Kerk Street and bounded by Jeppe, Pritchard, Harrison and Fraser Streets (north, south, east and west respectively) [43 D8]
CLIENT First National Bank
ASSOCIATE ARCHITECTS GAPP Architects & Urban Designers, Meyer Pienaar Architects & Urban Designers, RFB Architects
STRUCTURAL ENGINEER Ove Arup Inc.
CONTRACT VALUE R431 million
SIZE 200,000 square metres
GETTING THERE bus 10, 22, 34, 62, 63, 67 or 79
ACCESS ground-floor retail areas open; access to office levels is restricted

Revel Fox & Partners 1995

Central Johannesburg

Revel Fox & Partners 1995

Civic Spine

The principal aim of this development was to bring life to an increasingly soulless CBD by giving focus and symbolism to the city's Civic Spine – an axial sequence of public spaces between the Library, City Hall and the Post Office. Made up of two site components, the project was the subject of controversy right from the start.

The first and least contentious of the interventions is in Civic Square, which forms the city's 'Sacred Heart' and which is defined by the City Hall and Rissik Street Post Office. The design focuses on the Post Office (formerly the region's seat of government), the city's most historic building, from which distances from Johannesburg are measured. Radial lines in the square's paving design emanate from this central point, drawing attention to the Post Office building. The two obelisk-like structures standing sentinel in front of the Post Office were originally meant to support giant gates that would shut traffic out of the square – a well-intentioned but half-baked idea subsequently scrapped in favour of free traffic flow. The street is divided by a fountain symbolising the Witwatersrand; this slows the traffic flow and, combined with the vestigial gate posts, makes crossing between the square and the Post Office something of an obstacle course.

The more controversial part of the project was the enclosure of the Library gardens. Divided in two by a major street, the gardens are defined at each end by the Library and City Hall. The layout of the scheme extends the axial symmetry suggested by these neo-classical buildings (but perversely does not allow axial approach to either of them) and attempts to link the two halves of the gardens by camouflaging the street surface with brick paving (a footbridge would have done the trick better, and would have made crossing a lot safer for pedestrians).

Four gatehouses mark entrance points to the gardens and accommo-

Meyer Pienaar Architects & Urban Designers 1991

date stairwells to underground parking and public toilets. The gatehouse structures extend to form double-storey street walls which, running one third of the length between the Library and City Hall, house shops, space for flower stalls and access ramps to the parking. The upper levels of the wall accommodate a restaurant and a pub, each with a trellis-covered open area. The creation of these street walls came in for criticism, since they were thought to destroy motorists' enjoyment of the civic space. Also controversial was the decision to introduce formal commercial activities.

Detailing and finishes are as compromised as the project itself.

ADDRESS between Harrison, President, Rissik and Market Streets [44 B1]
CLIENT Johannesburg City Council
STRUCTURAL ENGINEER BKS Inc.
CONTRACT VALUE R10.5 million
SIZE three city blocks
GETTING THERE bus 81, 82, 27, 60, 61, 31, 44A, 45, 46, 56, 73, 74A, 80, 80B, 62 or 63 to Rissik Street Post Office
ACCESS open

Meyer Pienaar Architects & Urban Designers 1991

Meyer Pienaar Architects & Urban Designers 1991

Gencor Building

This building houses the corporate headquarters of Gencor, a company formed when two mining corporations founded before the turn of the century – the General Mining and Finance Company and Union Corporation – merged in 1980. Like many of the country's large mining companies, Gencor diversified in the mid-1980s to offset the effects of a faltering gold industry. The purpose of this design was therefore to provide an envelope for a variety of individually functioning corporate entities while expressing a unified image for Gencor as a whole.

Taking up a whole city block in downtown Johannesburg, the project integrates five existing buildings into its design. The most significant of these are the modernist 1950s General Mining Building (GMB) and the art deco Harcourt House, both of which were partly retained and which occupy the site's southern edge and south-east corner respectively.

Designed to respond to the individual characters of their surrounding streets, the building's façades present four distinct dynamics: transparency comes into play on the high-profile northern elevation; stature and solidity represent the predominantly traditional façade on to the more insular Hollard Street to the south; and there is an interplay of various forms on the east and west façades. The curved planes here hint at the building's internal geometry which is made up of circular fabric enclosing a ten-storey light-filled atrium.

From the Hollard Street entrance, a direct route through the GMB foyer leads up twin escalators to the atrium's vast public piazza on the first floor. Far from being a passive void, the space is lively and busy, ringed by a range of amenities (including a restaurant, automatic teller/cashpoint machine, media centre and auditorium). The piazza is also a main circulation route: rather than having to circumnavigate the entire building, workers can simply cross the piazza at floor level or via overhead bridges

Taljaard Carter Architects 1995

Taljaard Carter Architects 1995

linking lift access to all floors. Splashes of colour enliven otherwise plain white interiors, embellishing the glossy granite floor and indicating key circulation points. The water features and planting so often found in office buildings are here kept to a discreet minimum, so that the overall feeling is fresh, crisp and blissfully uncluttered. The atrium rooflight is a strengthened steel structure which, while casting interesting shadows into the space below, also has the rather more important function of containing the possible fall of an aircraft from the adjacent heliport.

The need to increase the building's bulk on the main elevation gave rise to some interesting structural manoeuvring. Unable to carry the load, a freestanding column at the building's south-west corner acts as an alternative support for a ring beam from which three storeys of new fabric are hung. The beam curves around the building at roof level, weaving through each corner.

This project makes a superb job of bringing historical design paradigms together with an essentially modern aesthetic, allowing each language expression within a single entity.

ADDRESS 6 Hollard Street [43 B8]
CLIENT Gencor SA Ltd
STRUCTURAL ENGINEER Ellmer Partnership Inc.
GLASS MANUFACTURER PFG Building Glass (Pty) Ltd
CONTRACT VALUE R110 million
SIZE 32,000 square metres
GETTING THERE bus 55,57, 52, 52A, 54 or 56 to the corner of Main and Simmonds Streets
ACCESS by appointment (contact Nico van Jaarsveld on 011 376 9111)

Taljaard Carter Architects 1995

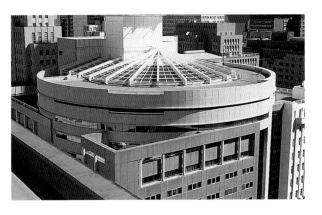

Central Johannesburg

Taljaard Carter Architects 1995

Commissioner Street upgrade

This scheme consists of a series of minimal urban interventions spanning eight blocks in Johannesburg's Central Business District. Conceived of by the council as a pilot project, it involved the introduction of bollards, benches, planting, paving and crossings. It also included the provision of stalls for hawkers, going some way to address the controversial issue of informal trading, which has reached almost epidemic proportions (one survey estimated that there were 11,000 hawkers operating in Johannesburg's CBD). Thirty of the 105 hawkers identified on this patch of the city had licensed stalls through private initiatives; the plan was therefore to accommodate the remaining 75.

Close liaison with land owners, tenants and the hawkers themselves enabled the architects to establish specific stall positions, with allowances made for denser groupings on more popular sites. Backing on to the street side of the pavement and anchored in a concrete foundation, the stalls' tubular steel frames provide support for demountable plank shelving and cantilevered fabric canopies.

The project includes two other interesting aspects: the 16-metre diameter circular pattern of the pedestrian crossing, best appreciated from the upper storeys of the adjacent buildings; and the 60 or so carved bollards which punctuate the scheme's length.

ADDRESS Commissioner Street (between Delvers and Rissik Streets) [44 B1]
CLIENT Greater Johannesburg Transitional Metropolitan Council, Metropolitan Services Delivery
GETTING THERE bus 27,31, 43, 44, 44A, 45, 46,56, 60,61, 62 or 63 to Commissioner Street
ACCESS open

Central Johannesburg

Informal Sector Consultants 1995

Central Johannesburg

Informal Sector Consultants 1995

55 Marshall Street

This office tower joins a family of historical buildings owned by the Anglo American Corporation which, occupying 44 and 45 Main Street, represent the most significant historic enclave in the city.

Culminating in a copper cross-barrel vault, the 18-storey tower rises proudly above its predecessors. It incorporates basement parking, a computer centre, and dining facilities on the top floor. The spaces within the vaults house the plant of the building.

That Johannesburg favourite, the skywalk, bridges Ferreira Street to connect the tower with Anglo American's head office at 44 Main Street. The tower's massive, sandstone-clad façade makes material reference to the head office building, carrying through its proportions in the design of the window elements. The overall impression sets the tower firmly in the fold, a powerful addition to the complex as a whole.

Central Johannesburg

ADDRESS 55 Marshall Street [43 B8]
CLIENT Anglo American Corporation
STRUCTURAL ENGINEER Ove Arup Inc.
CONTRACT VALUE R150 million
SIZE 32,300 square metres
GETTING THERE bus 2, 2A, 2B, 14, 19, 19A, 20, 20A, 33, 71, 71A, 78, 80, 81 or 82 to Main Street at the Magistrates' Court terminus
ACCESS none

RFB Architects 1994

RFB Architects 1994

Johannesburg Art Gallery extensions

To complete the unfinished work of a great architect and significantly to enlarge a closed composition – this was the daunting task for the architects of the Johannesburg Art Gallery extensions. As the final evolutionary phase of Sir Edwin Lutyens' design (1911), the scheme had also to reconcile the gallery with its park setting, unacknowledged by the original work which was oriented away from the gardens toward the city.

The architect's response comprises two major parts: an extension above ground which follows the axial footprint of the existing building, completing it by adding two wings and a portico fronting the park; and a sunken gallery space housing the bulk of accommodation not fitting into the composition. The two wings, echoing the form and proportions of the original, define new courts and give stature to the gallery's ends. The King George Street approach is particularly successful in establishing a sense of place. Here passers-by are presented with a sculpture court set behind a small public square providing the access link to the park and gallery. Packed with vendors, the area acts as an extension of the bustling street mall skirting the park edge. Within, the new portico bleeds into the gardens with a forecourt, fountains and ramps.

The real challenge of this project is that it inherently demanded an interpretation of classicism. The wings are a clear yet individual continuation of the existing elements while the portico, a post-modern rendition, carries through lines and motifs as shadows of their classical selves: the cornice is a flattened band, and the arches, isolated gestures.

Careful choice of material (face brick, coursed to make reference to the original sandstone), proportions and articulation ensure that the overall effect is a harmonious fusion with the old. What lets the show down is the sunken gallery. This, intended to quietly complement, simply compromises the garden façade. Its long, copper-clad rooflights form

Central Johannesburg

Meyer Pienaar Architects & Urban Designers 1991

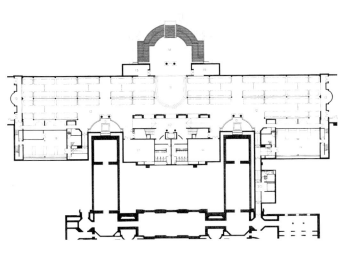

Meyer Pienaar Architects & Urban Designers 1991

vaulted tracks truncating the façade and obscuring its monumentality. Whatever your viewpoint the wings, portico and Lutyens' end façades look decidedly cramped.

Inside the gallery, long flat interiors come as a surprise and disappointment after the external promise of lofty spaces. Due to economic necessity, accommodation within the volumes is stacked and the vaulted ceilings largely concealed by technical consoles (the barrel-vaulted spaces are only experienced in less public spaces and the portico cafeteria). A sequence of sunken courts with dramatic exterior views provides some compensation.

Central Johannesburg

ADDRESS in Joubert Park public gardens, Klein Street [44 A1]
CLIENT Johannesburg City Council
STRUCTURAL ENGINEER BKS Inc.
SIZE 5500 square metres
GETTING THERE bus 18, 49A (Saturday only), 27, 46 to Joubert Park
ACCESS open Tuesday to Sunday 10.00–17.00 (closed Mondays); admission free

Meyer Pienaar Architects & Urban Designers 1991

Meyer Pienaar Architects & Urban Designers 1991

Cactusland

Cactusland is a company that distributes cacti from nursery to retail outlets. This building, a transitional point for the temporary housing, repackaging and display of the plants, is more than your average storage shed. Situated on a prominent corner site within the city grid pattern of New Doornfontein, it is bounded by a busy four-lane road carrying traffic southwards off the highway, and surrounded by large, dominant buildings. The architect has exploited this context to extend the notion of display into the design of the building itself, which takes its cue from the morphology of the cactus plant. It is not altogether surprising that this project, characterised by exaggerated wall thickness and an angular roof plane, has the unmistakable quality of an urban folly.

Consisting of two distinct sections, the building rises to its highest point at the head of the intersection where its presence is asserted by the bulbous, insular form of the main office and reception area. Its adjacent box volume, which provides flexible space and service facilities, is opened up with large display windows along the street edge. Both segments contain isolated mezzanine levels.

ADDRESS 62 Beit Street (corner with Sivewright Avenue), New Doornfontein [44 A1]
CLIENT Cactusland
STRUCTURAL ENGINEER Mark Axelrod
CONTRACT VALUE R350,000
SIZE 212 square metres
GETTING THERE bus 27
ACCESS open

Heather Dodd Architect 1996

Heather Dodd Architect 1996

Central Johannesburg

Johannesburg Athletics Stadium

One of the first projects to be undertaken after the 1994 elections, this stadium was conceived as part of Johannesburg's bid to host the 2004 Olympic Games. It also provided a catalyst for the regeneration of the Ellis Park precinct, its surrounding inner city area.

In the arid highveld landscape, the stadium forms a crater cradled in the valley formed by the meeting of Yeoville and Kensington Ridges, with the Central Business District as its western backdrop. Its eastward orientation follows the slope of the site, maximising the usage time of the stadium and creating an ideal venue for afternoon events.

The stadium is an oval arena within a circular perimeter. Creating varying scales within, the shallow bowl of the amphitheatre rises in a sweeping curve to form the main stand at its high western end. The huge, elegantly curved canopy sheltering the area provides the dramatic high-point of this design. Its structure is a lightweight steel deck whose complex form is a segment of a vault with an internal radius of some 300 metres. The canopy is suspended from six triangular steel masts, their design intended to make reference to Johannesburg's mining tradition. The supporting system is entirely in tension, with each mast leaning forwards against the grandstand's concrete substructure (stadium bowl) via a pair of thrust beams, the junction between concrete and steel bearing their load.

Varying in height around the bowl, the masts mark the entrances. Their triangular structures integrate spiral ramps, providing access to the various levels of the grandstand and in turn to a public concourse in the form of a lip skirting the bowl's outer rim along the lower south, east and north extremes of the stadium. The ramps located at the north and south ends of the bowl shelter 2000 square metres of office space (one of the features that make this stadium a more active part of city life than those

Arup Associates 1995

Arup Associates 1995

that are open only a couple of times a week). Another of the scheme's contributions to urban life is a warm-up track which has a direct link to the bowl. Also built to international standards but without extensive seating, it can be used by the local community.

While stadiums are always in danger of becoming anonymous formula buildings, this one represents a contextually sensitive design appropriately built with local resources and materials.

ADDRESS Ellis Park, New Doornfontein [44 A3]
PROJECT ARCHITECT James Burland, Ove Arup London
ASSOCIATE ARCHITECT RFB Architects
CLIENT Greater Johannesburg Transitional Metropolitan Council; Johannesburg Administration (Sport & Recreation)
STRUCTURAL ENGINEER Ove Arup Johannesburg
CONTRACT VALUE R97 million
GETTING THERE from the centre of town head north towards Braamfontein until you reach Smit Street (M10 east). Travel eastwards on Smit Street (becomes Saratoga) and then under the bridge where it becomes Charlton. From the bridge turn right at the second set of traffic lights into Van Beek Street and you will see the stadium on your right
ACCESS open

Arup Associates 1995

Central Johannesburg

Arup Associates 1995

Johannesburg suburbs

Saunders Street housing

Located in a cosmopolitan area that has generally been side-stepped by banks and developers, these two separate developments present attractive low-cost models for urban living. The first to be built was the architect's own home, which occupies a single plot. Designed as an architectural experiment, it combines affordability and innovation by using steel-frame construction. The adjacent row of housing consists of three units and offers an alternative model to the freestanding house and apartment blocks which characterise the city. Here, traditional cross-wall construction is used, with the units built simultaneously. Collectively these units – all of single-room width and four levels high – form what the architect calls 'a habitable garden wall'.

Bedrooms are on the second floor and loft level, while kitchen and dining areas are on the first floor with a double-volume living space and garage facilities on a split-level ground floor. In contrast to the street façade's minimal fenestration, the north elevation which faces on to a secure garden area is heavily glazed, creating warm, light-filled interiors.

Johannesburg suburbs

ADDRESS 47 and 49 Saunders Street, Yeoville
CLIENTS Jeff Stacey and Annie Smythe
STRUCTURAL ENGINEER L S C Brunette & Partners
CONTRACT VALUE R300,000 (no. 47); R100,000 (no. 49)
SIZE no. 47: 140 square metres per unit, 420 square metres total; no. 49: 180 square metres
GETTING THERE south from Raleigh Street by five blocks, between Fortesque and Kenmere Streets
ACCESS by appointment (telephone the architects on 011 482 2323)

Jeff Stacey & Associates Architects 1989

Jeff Stacey & Associates Architects 1989

22 Girton Road

This building and Helmut Jahn's other contribution to the city ('The Diamond' in the Central Business District, see page 138) present an interesting paradox. In the CBD, where the streets teem with pedestrians, he created a latter-day fortress. Here in Parktown, where virtually no one goes about on foot, he has created a powerful experience for pedestrians.

Four levels of office space, curved in a horseshoe shape, enclose a glazed public courtyard which, with its palm trees, reflecting pond and structural steelwork, brings to mind an enormous Victorian conservatory. Fronting balconied upper levels, a colonnade of columns supports the roof structure which is 23 metres tall at its highest point, with arches spanning the 30-metre width. One of the trickiest parts of construction was the peak of the semicircle where 11 radial arches converge at a single point. Underground parking rids this building of the 'parking lot' feel common to many other Parktown offices. It also creates a platform which, level with Girton Road, provides the main approach. Pedestrian entry is directly into the open end of the horseshoe, while vehicle access is via punctured openings in the platform edge. A two-storey-high opening through the rear of the enclosure frames the view of the Braamfontein Ridge in the distance.

ADDRESS 22 Girton Road, Parktown [35 D8]
CLIENT Anglo American Property Services (AMPROS)
ASSOCIATE ARCHITECT Kemp Brooksbank
STRUCTURAL ENGINEER Ove Arup Inc.
CONTRACT VALUE R22 million SIZE 8150 square metres
GETTING THERE take bus 71, 72, 73, 82, 83, 84 or 85 to the junction of Empire and Hillside Roads. Hillside Road, becomes Girton Road
ACCESS courtyard open, but access to offices restricted

Murphy/Jahn 1985

Murphy/Jahn 1985

Westcliff house and cottages

The development of this three-unit residential complex followed in the wake of a town-planning amendment which allowed owners of single-residence sites to build a main house plus two additional cottages of up to 110 square metres each.

The buildings are situated on the lower reaches of Westcliff Ridge on a sharply sloping rectangular site bounded by roads at either end. Currently used as the architects' own offices, the single-storey cottage on the lower end of the site is the more introverted of the three buildings. It is symmetrically planned, with two wings of cellular accommodation flanking an open-plan central area accessed through an entrance courtyard. An existing stone wall shields the building from the busy traffic of its adjacent road. By contrast, the boldly cubic façades of the double-storey main house and the second cottage inch right up to the edge of their quiet, tree-lined suburban street, commanding views across the valley. Both these units are characterised by rich, earthy tones and common elements such as twin chimneys, bay windows and steep shingle roofs which make reference to the Arts and Crafts houses of their surrounding environment. Natural materials and finishes such as slate, tile, timber and coir covering are used throughout.

ADDRESS 48 Westcliff Drive and 43 Crescent Drive, Westcliff [35 C7]
CLIENT Crescent Drive Properties
STRUCTURAL ENGINEER Philip Badenhorst
CONTRACT VALUE R2 million
SIZE 600 square metres
GETTING THERE take the M1 highway north; after the Saint Andrews turn-off, turn into Loch Avenue. This becomes Westcliff Drive
ACCESS by appointment (telephone Alfio Torrisi on 011 486 1815)

Alfio Torrisi Architects 1995

Johannesburg suburbs

Alfio Torrisi Architects 1995

House Staude

Situated high on a ridge in the trendy northern suburb of Melville, this is a small single-storey house which has been converted into a home and office for the client's creative publishing business. The transformation, described by the client as 'Cinderella into Cindy Crawford', has left the retained original house virtually unrecognisable. Fondly referred to as the 'shack sensation', this is an eclectic concoction of exuberant forms with materials mostly left in their natural state – oxidised plaster, timber, Rhinolite, colourful mosaics, wrought iron and corrugated-iron sheeting.

A lower-level approach reveals the house's rock foundation and presents the street with two separate entrances – a curved ramp to the house proper and a stepped side alley to its office component and staff cottage. Perched above, the house makes playful reference to its surroundings: an additional level in timber, clad with corrugated iron, recalls the corrugated-iron-framed structures historically used in the area; the floating, undulating roof echoes the surrounding hills. The wavy lines of the roof are reiterated at the cut-off point to the ground floor and in the balcony which shelters the main entrance.

Internally, double volumes, layered spaces and high windows give a sense of spaciousness to tight and efficient planning. The interior design achieves a delicate balance between spontaneously crafted and sophisticatedly sleek.

ADDRESS 34 Eighth Avenue (off Fourth Street), Melville [35 D5]
CLIENT Ingrid Staude
STRUCTURAL ENGINEER Jan Rosnovanu
SIZE 356 square metres
GETTING THERE take bus 67 to Fourth Avenue, Melville
ACCESS by appointment (telephone 011 426 2338)

Kate Otten Architect 1995

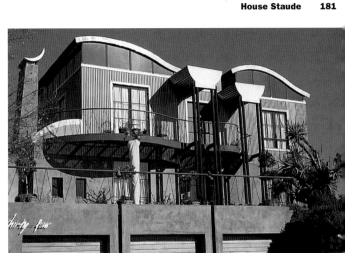

Kate Otten Architect 1995

Hyatt Hotel

A massive square-windowed wall manoeuvres around the corner of Oxford Road and Biermann Avenue. Its expression is neutral, its adornment minimal. This is the chilly public face of the Hyatt Group's first South African hotel, heralded by the architects and architectural journals as a 'contemporary African design'. The design is 'an attempt to look at architecture afresh and from first principles... stripping away the trappings of our colonial past'.

It is without a doubt a well-executed modern building, a bold statement flying in the face of the prevailing retro trend. But reinventing Rossi rationalism as African – really!

Johannesburg suburbs

ADDRESS corner of Oxford Road and
 Biermann Avenue, Rosebank [28 E1]
CLIENT Iscor Pension Fund
STRUCTURAL ENGINEER Arup Consulting
Engineers
CONTRACT VALUE R60 million
SIZE 16,000 square metres
GETTING THERE take bus 1, 2, 2A, 4 or 87
ACCESS public areas open

GAPP Architects & Urban Designers 1996

Johannesburg suburbs

GAPP Architects & Urban Designers 1996

Cradock Heights

Cradock Heights is a commercial development designed by London-based architect Stephen Le Roith in collaboration with his father's South African-based practice, Harold Le Roith & Associates.

On a corner site at an intersection occupied by three financial institutions, the premises were developed in the hope of attracting two banking tenants, thus establishing this as a mini(scule) financial centre. Two parallel self-contained wings linked by a glass atrium space provide wide banking halls at ground level, with narrower ancillary offices on the two levels above. These rectangular wings are staggered relative to each other, with the southerly wing slipping forwards so that it abuts the street.

Above ground level the floors peel back to provide generous east-facing terraces, creating a sleek, elegant profile which emphasises the horizontality of the building. Narrower setbacks on the upper floors of the north elevations carry framed grilles which act as sun-control devices and contribute to the building's hi-tech aesthetic. The light-drenched interior is animated by a glass elevator and steel bridges which make circulation to upper levels and between wings a joy. The extensive glazing and refined steelwork give an air of exquisite delicacy which contrasts with the weight and solidity of the exposed concrete skeletal structure.

ADDRESS 21 Cradock Avenue (corner Tyrwitt Avenue), Rosebank [28 E1]
CLIENT Cradock Heights Pty Ltd
STRUCTURAL ENGINEER Ove Arup Inc.
CONTRACT VALUE R13 million SIZE 3500 square metres
GETTING THERE N1 north from central Johannesburg. Take the Glenhove off-ramp and turn left for Rosebank; at junction of Glenhove and Oxford Roads go straight into Bolton Road. Take first left into Cradock Avenue
ACCESS to the atrium only

Harold H Le Roith & Associates, Stephen Le Roith Architects 1991

Johannesburg suburbs

Harold H Le Roith & Associates, Stephen Le Roith Architects 1991

The Pavilion

This building is nestled in the garden of a private residential property in the well-established suburb of Melrose. Designed as a recreational pavilion, it provides the client with a place to entertain guests who come to play tennis on the adjacent court, or to swim in the small pool in the pavilion itself (a larger pool once occupied this corner of the garden).

Poised on a raised area which acts as a podium, the building is articulated by a minimal planar composition: two intersecting and overlapping roof planes hover above a combination of freestanding and supporting curved and splaying bagged white walls. This Miesian composition is defined by the existing L-shaped garden wall. As with Mies' Barcelona Pavilion – the key influence of this design – the approach is a subtle celebration of the experience of arrival. An axial walkway from the eastern street entrance is deflected to steps perpendicular to the south-facing main façade. One's perspective is thus subtly shifted so that elements are revealed only gradually. It is a powerful and seductive device. On arrival at the top of the stairs one finds oneself in a transitional zone contained by the lower and narrower of the two roof planes. Running the length of the façade, this covered walkway is terminated physically and visually by a square section pier housing a pizza oven. Above, the broader, cantilevered roof overshoots the enclosed areas to provide a generous canopy sheltering an outdoor seating area.

Inside, the space is punctuated by sculptural forms: a top-lit partial cylinder encases a spiral staircase leading to a wine cellar (formerly the deep end of the swimming pool, whose retained slope adds a charming touch); curved lines are followed through in the bar counter and its containing wall; a play of restrained diagonals defines service areas at the far end of the space. The backdrop to these gestures is a steel column and beam structure following a 4-metre module. One of the columns is clev-

Peter Rich Architect 1992

Peter Rich Architect 1992

erly concealed in a small, red-painted cylinder which punctures the floor plate to provide the cellar with ventilation and act as a vessel transporting sounds between the cellar and the main room when parties are in swing.

The clean lines and balanced proportions of this pavilion owe much to the well-detailed slender roofs – a mere 150 millimetres incorporating flush ceilings. Large glass panels designed to slide away into wall cavities link inside and outside, a connection accentuated by the consistent use of slate tiles (a reference to the fabric of the main house) for the stairs, walkway and internal room, with only a small rise in floor level to demarcate the change of domain.

This pavilion's clarity of design and detailing is sophisticated simplicity at its best.

Johannesburg suburbs

ADDRESS 15 Arran Avenue, Melrose [28 D2]
ASSOCIATE ARCHITECT Kevin Fellingham
CLIENT Vivienne Mennell
STRUCTURAL ENGINEER Jan Cizek
SIZE 100 square metres
ACCESS by appointment (telephone the architect on 011 726 6151)

Peter Rich Architect 1992

Peter Rich Architect 1992

Saheti Primary School

The overriding image of this private Greek primary school is of a rambling, miniature village. Its key concession to formality is a planted amphitheatre which, like a typical village square, is the focus for communal activities and a reference point for visitors. Set behind this, the school's structure appears to embrace its surrounding landscape.

Organisation relies on a flexible three-dimensional system which allows for extensions and adjustments to be made without the school ever seeming unfinished or incomplete. Internally, the deep space arrangement eliminates wasteful and possibly hostile access corridors in favour of interconnecting open-plan teaching areas. These are fixed within a tartan grid plan of 'master' spaces (classrooms) and 'servant' spaces (service aisles accommodating storage, toilets and seating bays) expressed by pitched tiled roofs and flat concrete slabs respectively. Orientated in different directions, the clerestoried roofs give the building a figurative animation while individually providing classrooms with ventilation and light of varying intensity.

Circulation routes weave in and out of classrooms, where the atmosphere is boisterous yet controlled. Surprisingly, rather than being a recipe for kiddy chaos, the fluid spatial arrangement seems to have engendered an unusual degree of self-discipline among the children.

ADDRESS Wordsworth Avenue, Senderwood [38 A3]
CLIENT Saheti School Parent Teachers Association
STRUCTURAL ENGINEER P Manias & Partners
GETTING THERE take the M2 east. Proceed on to the N3 to Pretoria and take the Edenvale off-ramp. Turn left and travel for approximately 1 kilometre. Wordsworth Avenue is to your left
ACCESS by appointment (telephone Denae on 011 453 8210)

Fassler Kamstra Architects 1980

Johannesburg suburbs

Fassler Kamstra Architects 1980

Sandton and Randburg

House Malelane

South Africa has much of the technology that one expects to find in the advanced construction industries of Western countries. Unlike in these countries, however, it is not usually available for anything but the largest building contracts. This house, an exhilarating union of hi-tech and nature, is an exception to the rule, bringing technological expertise into the domestic realm. It will doubtless become a landmark domestic building.

Designed as an urban retreat, the house is situated on a sloping one-acre site in the exclusive northern suburb of Hyde Park. A tree-lined access avenue weaving through the site separates the house from the adjacent studio. In plan, the joint configuration of these two units is a parallelogram, slanted at 15 degrees so that it relates to the site and orientates the main house due north. The house is a glass pavilion with a light, filigree structure. Recessed floor-to-ceiling glass provides the containing envelope above which hovers a slender, sinusoidal roof plate suspended from an external steel structure. With the dissolution of external walls, house and studio become like private courtyards defined by shrubs, trees and the surrounding garden wall.

The building's massive, undulating roof is a spectacular feature, appearing remarkably thin at 250 millimetres. A 20 x 30-metre parallelogram, it consists of steel grillage topped with lightweight concrete for insulation and additional rigidity. Waterproofing is provided by an externally applied membrane. Its supporting frame is both structure and architecture: V-struts and booms, held in a cat's cradle of ties, form asymmetric pylons which stand poised in dynamic tension at each corner of the roof. The booms from which the house is hung are themselves suspended, tethered to the V-struts. The studio roof plate uses the same structural system as the main house. Here, the roof is supported jointly by steel columns

Stephen Le Roith Architects 1997

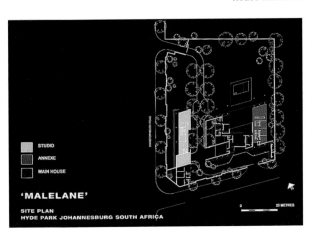

STUDIO

ANNEXE

MAIN HOUSE

'MALELANE'

SITE PLAN
HYDE PARK JOHANNESBURG SOUTH AFRICA

0   25 METRES

Sandton and Randburg

Stephen Le Roith Architects 1997

and load-bearing walls.

Internally, the house has a skewed U-shaped plan that can be subdivided to give two independent spaces – the main bedroom wing and central living area, and a self-contained annexe for use by the client's extended family (guests are accommodated in the two-bedroom self-contained studio). A glazed conservatory not only forms a transitional space between the outside terrace and living area but also provides the house's main energy-saving feature, expelling hot air through skylights and drawing cool air into the interior spaces.

Finishes focus on a small palette of neutral colours, with materials including steel, ceramic tiles, polished granite and oak.

ADDRESS 26 Christopherson Road, Hyde Park [27 C8]
CLIENT Lilian Le Roith Investments cc.
STRUCTURAL ENGINEER Arup (Pty) Ltd SA
SIZE 415 square metres (house); 157 square metres (studio); 62 square metres (staff accommodation)
GETTING THERE proceed north on the N1 highway from Johannesburg city centre. Take the Corlett Drive off-ramp (also sign-posted to the Wanderers cricket ground) and drive towards Rosebank. Turn right at the junction with Oxford Road then take the first right into Hurlingham Road. The house is at the corner of Hurlingham and Christopherson Roads
ACCESS by appointment (telephone Harold H. Le Roith & Associates on 011 788 7216)

Sandton and Randburg

Stephen Le Roith Architects 1997

Stephen Le Roith Architects 1997

Velocity film studios

Home to Velocity Films, a leading production company, this two-storey, linear 'Dream Factory' houses production suites, video libraries, recording rooms and so on, all organised around a top-lit double-volume internal street which broadens to a canteen at its end. Noero's approach, marked by an engaging functionalism, has responded to the client's desire for a building that can be viewed as a 'work in progress' similar to a film set and that can over time change to accommodate new needs.

A steel structural frame dominates the building, both inside and out, with all other materials – brick, timber, corrugated roof sheeting and concrete – mostly left unfinished, playing a subordinate role as infill panels or freestanding forms. Components are conventional and fittings off-the-shelf. There is a clear hierarchy between the building's two levels: activities directly related to film production are on the more robust and rugged ground level, while the administrative level above is more refined, with timber flooring and dry-wall instead of brick walling.

The sloping site is surrounded by deciduous trees which provide shade in summer and allow north light into the offices in winter. The informal quality of the roof echoes farm buildings and old mining sheds.

ADDRESS 38 Wessels Road, Rivonia [12 C3]
CLIENT Velocity Afrika
STRUCTURAL ENGINEER Sam Carsons
CONTRACT VALUE R1.9 million SIZE 900 square metres
GETTING THERE take the Rivonia Road turn-off from the N1; head south on Rivonia Road and turn left at the first traffic lights. Turn at the bend into Wessels Road. Cross the four-way stop. The building is on the left-hand side in the middle of the next block
ACCESS by appointment (telephone Melanie Sinton on 011 807 0100)

Jo Noero Architects 1996

Jo Noero Architects 1996

Herdbuoys head office

In a predominantly industrial area on the outskirts of Johannesburg, this renovated warehouse accommodates the corporate headquarters of Herdbuoys Advertising. The brief called for an Afrocentric design interpreted through colour, texture, form and materials with a local reference.

The building is essentially a square-plan, double-storey block sliced through at an angle by a triple-volume spine containing the principal circulation route and internal stairwell. Finished in saturated African Red, the spine is presented externally as a monumental split column dividing the main façade into two – a double-height glazed Winblok wall on one side and a curtain wall providing the entrance on the other. All the wall planes are deeply recessed, highlighting the interplay between the focal 'column' and an exaggerated roof beam framing the façade. From outside, the effect is simple and dramatic.

Inside, a lofty foyer space feeds off to the naturally lit corridor bounded on either side by cellular offices and boardroom facilities. Despite a tight budget, the inventive use of low-cost materials creates a sophisticated corporate environment. Bright wall colours bring richness while inspired features such as the perforated-metal light fittings add coherence.

Sandton and Randburg

ADDRESS corner 14th Street and Fifth Avenue, Malboro North [21 C7]
CLIENT Herdbuoys Advertising Agency
STRUCTURAL ENGINEER GBG Hodson
CONTRACT VALUE R1.2 million SIZE 1200 square metres
GETTING THERE take the M1 north. Turn right off the motorway into Marlboro Drive; proceed for approximately 800 metres and turn left into Fifth Avenue (just after the JSN car showroom). The building is at the first corner/junction ACCESS open 8.00–17.00 (telephone in advance for an appointment, 011 444 8844)

Julius & Company 1995

Julius & Company 1995

Sandton Square

Sandton is a northern enclave of Johannesburg, a bastion of white bourgeois lifestyle that placidly revolves around shopping malls, office parks and fortified villas. A place where everyone goes everywhere by car, it has a sanitised, dislocated feel similar to that of an North American suburb. Its centre, paradoxically known as Sandton City, is a commercial core that lacked a focal point to attract pedestrians.

Commissioned by the town council to create a civic focus, the architects took as their model the Italian piazza, interpreting it literally in a full-scale mock-up – a plaza containing great slabs of stage-set neo-classicism offering a mixture of shops, offices and restaurants.

Architecturally, this is an easy project to criticise, yet its retrogressive expression is part of a broader cultural phenomenon: classicism, with its European associations, offers a security blanket, giving middle-class whites a feeling of sanity in a siege society.

The development is linked to Sandton City via a 30-metre-wide shopping mall, creating the largest continuous shopping area in the country.

ADDRESS Sandton Square, Sandton [20 E2]
ASSOCIATE ARCHITECTS Bental Abramson & Partners, GAPP Architects & Urban Designers
CLIENT Sandton Town Council
STRUCTURAL ENGINEER Leech Price Associates
CONTRACT VALUE R350 million SIZE 146,000 square metres
GETTING THERE take the M1 north. Turn off at the Grayston Drive exit; proceed for approximately 3.5 kilometres and after the West Street junction turn left into 5th Street
ACCESS open

Sandton and Randburg

Meyer Pienaar Architects & Urban Designers 1995

Meyer Pienaar Architects & Urban Designers 1995

Sandton Library and Art Gallery

Accommodating a library and the chambers of the Sandton town council as well as an affiliated art gallery, this building is part of a grand vision to give the stylistically schizoid commercial sprawl of Sandton a sense of civic place. Occupying a pivotal position within the development, it stands on an awkward wedge-shaped site straddling two dramatically different public squares – the *cinquecento*-style commercial plaza of Sandton Square to the west (see page 202), and a formal open space to the east. Set at an odd angle to each other and on different levels, the building's façades define one side of each square.

The building comprises three wings organised around a triangular internal courtyard – a symbolic intermediate square between the two large external squares. Two routes connect the squares: one leads through the building itself; the other is a colonnaded external walkway which, skirting the building's southern end, delineates the boundary of a tranquil sculpture garden fronting the small art gallery. With its trendy, cranked corrugated aluminium canopy, the walkway presents a playful contrast to the formal Kahnesque language of the building's façades. Both elevations are articulated by deep-set windows varying in size from double-volume, flat-arched openings on the ground floor to circular portholes on the top floor. On the eastern elevation, two cylindrical towers housing vertical circulation dominate the main entrance, lending an air of civic monumentality and grandeur.

ADDRESS corner West and Rivonia Roads, Sandton [20 E2]
CLIENT Sandton Town Council
STRUCTURAL ENGINEER Ove Arup & Partners
CONTRACT VALUE R17 million SIZE 4500 square metres
ACCESS open Monday to Thursday 9.00–19.00, Friday 9.00–18.00, Saturday 9.00–13.00, closed Sunday

GAPP Architects & Urban Designers 1994

GAPP Architects & Urban Designers 1994

Sonneblom film studios

This building belongs not so much to the mundane middle-class corner of Randburg in which it is set, but rather to the wider landscape, to the highvelds of Southern Africa.

The complex occupies its entire rectangular site. Because of a 3-metre drop in level, it appears from the street to be domestically scaled, fitting snugly in its residential context. Thick walls extending to the site's boundary on three sides accentuate the building's mass and give a fortress-like impression which is underlined by minimal detailing. Curved forms to the street soften the severity of expression with seductive breaks which give a hint of the world within. Through the enclosure of a gravelled parking yard, a narrow bridge-link over the fall of ground leads between the curves of two giant Zimbabwean-inspired drums buttressing the entrance. Inside, the distant view of Johannesburg's skyline is the first sight you see through the glazed double-volume courtyard around which the building is wrapped. A staircase within one of the drums connects the two floors of the complex.

ADDRESS 1 Ateljee Street, Randpark Ridge, Randburg [16 C3]
CLIENT Sonneblom Films (Pty) Ltd
STRUCTURAL ENGINEER Ove Arup Inc.
CONTRACT VALUE R2.05 million
SIZE 1620 square metres
GETTING THERE from Johannesburg to N1 (western bypass) take DF Malan M5 turn-off. Continue along DF Malan Drive (northerly direction) for 4 kilometres. Take left turn into Dale Lace Avenue and second right into Ateljee Street
ACCESS by appointment (contact Henda Taljaard on 011 794 2100 between 9.00–13.00 weekdays)

M & M Bell Architects 1992

Sandton and Randburg

M & M Bell Architects 1992

Midrand

PFG Glass Centre

This building is the product of what is, in South Africa, a rare event – a smoothly run and widely publicised national competition. The client, a leading glass manufacturing company, wanted a building that would showcase its products and serve as a forum for the exchange of information within the industry. The result is a rotating mass of angular forms frozen in mid-collision beside the N1 motorway. The design, clearly influenced by Gehry's Vitra Museum, engages passing motorists in a dynamic spectacle that responds to, and is amplified by, a shifting perspective.

The image of shards of glass generates the building's plan-form while various facets of the materials are selectively displayed – framed and embedded within solid white masonry. Skylights extruded at precarious angles and leaning walls with displaced openings bounce and diffuse daylight into the galleries.

An exhibition space occupying the centre of the building encloses a glazed garden court, open to the sky. Upper-level offices, screened by unframed glass, overhang the public core. Sadly, the interior spaces are not as dynamic as the building's exterior suggests. Be sure to take a stroll around before you enter.

ADDRESS Augrabies Road, Waterfall Park [7 C6]
DESIGN ARCHITECT Henri Comrie STRUCTURAL ENGINEER Ove Arup Inc.
GLASS MANUFACTURER PFG Building Glass (Pty) Ltd
CONTRACT VALUE R3.07 million
SIZE 1028 square metres
GETTING THERE take the N1 highway north. Exit at the Allandale Road (R561) off-ramp bearing west. Take the first right turn into Bekker Road. Waterfall Office Park is the first turning to your right
ACCESS open Monday to Thursday 8.00–16.30; Friday 8.00–15.00

Midrand

Taljaard Carter Architects 1995

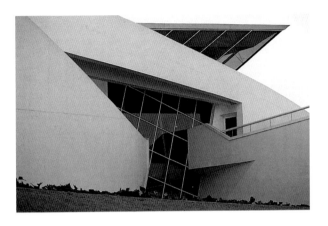

Taljaard Carter Architects 1995

Siemens Park

German electronics multinational Siemens marked the centenary of its formal corporate presence in South Africa with this massive headquarters complex. The first phase of a two-stage development, the complex consists of five L-shaped office blocks and a cylindrical tower. A further four blocks are in the pipeline. The design, intended to assert unequivocally the firm's technological leadership, was subjected to stringent specifications and overseen by a central in-house architectural unit. Not surprisingly, the result is unmistakably Meieresque (he designed Siemens' Munich office and his language of clinical precision is the one generally adopted by the firm). The complex's buildings are characterised by white powder-coated aluminium panels cladding walls and beams, with white-tinted off-shutter concrete columns supporting external sunscreens.

The complex is structured around an axial water feature flanked by promenades. Crossed by bridges along its length, the cascading feature culminates in a circular pond dominating the open plaza which serves as the principal pedestrian interchange. Emblazoned with the Siemens name, the silo-like tower is the complex's pivotal element, overshadowing its surrounding landscape. Beyond its entrance, which is marked by a suspended canopy, the view is of a gleaming white stepped canyon formed by the continuous façades of the office blocks.

ADDRESS 300 Janadel Avenue, Halfway House [7 B5]
CLIENT Siemens (Pty) Ltd SA
STRUCTURAL ENGINEER van Niekerk Kleyn & Edwards
CONTRACT VALUE R80 million (first phase)
GETTING THERE take the Allandale off-ramp from the N1 highway travelling north. Janadel Avenue is first on the right
ACCESS none

Midrand

Louw Apostolellis Bergenthuin Slee 1996

Louw Apostolellis Bergenthuin Slee 1996

Firmenich offices and factory

In an industrial/office park development in Midrand, this complex brings architecture into the domain of the themed container. Facilities for the client, a Swiss manufacturer of cosmetics and fragrances, include laboratories, test centres, offices and conference rooms.

The organisation of the office building follows a similar principle to that seen in an earlier Le Roith project, Cradock Heights: two parallel wings, staggered by one structural bay, flank a glass atrium bridged by a steel walkway. Placed diagonally across its site, the two-storey building addresses the corner of 16th Street and Pharmaceutical Road where the wings' chamfered corners direct attention to the main entrance across a landscaped court. This orientation called for massive shading devices which, combined with the steel roof construction, give the building its gull-wing character. Façades are clad in powder-coated aluminium and extensively glazed. Designed to extend across the site with a further phased development, the building will eventually connect to the neighbouring factory component with a glass link.

ADDRESS corner 16th Street and Pharmaceutical Road [7 A7]
ASSOCIATE ARCHITECT Stephen Le Roith Architects
STRUCTURAL ENGINEER Steve Stories & Associates
CONTRACT VALUE R10.6 million
SIZE 3999 square metres (factory); 1905 square metres (offices)
GETTING THERE from the N1 highway north, take the Olifantsfontein off-ramp. At the top of the off-ramp turn right at the junction with the R101 (the old Pretoria Road). Proceed along the R101 and at the first set of traffic lights turn right into George Road; proceed until the first four-way stop and turn left into 16th Street
ACCESS public areas open

Harold H Le Roith & Associates 1997

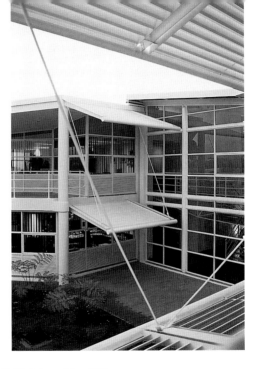

Harold H Le Roith & Associates 1997

Grand Central Water Tower

This gravity-defying, cone-shaped structure serves both as a water tower and a public sculpture. Standing 45 metres high, the cone is sited in the middle of the six-lane boulevard planned as the gateway to Halfway House, a new town in Midrand. Ten times the size of your common mushroom variety, the tower is the largest in the southern hemisphere.

Approaching the tower is an unnerving experience. Because of its outward lean, the closer you get to it, the larger it looms. Its 30-metre-wide top tapers to a mere 4 metres at ground level, where it stands off-centre in a circular pond. Just below the waterline, the head kinks straight down like a wine glass into a large, underground concrete base. Painted black, the base appears almost invisible, making the enormous structure above it seem weightless, as if hovering above the pond. Only the top of the tower is filled with water; its lower portion is kept hollow to provide the pressure required to raise it to the right height. Punctured with random openings, the hollow section is accessed via a bridge-link near the bottom of the tower. At the centre of the sloping volume there is a spiral staircase wrapped around a concrete service shaft which spirals through the water-filled level to emerge on a concrete deck at the 'top' of the cone.

ADDRESS Grand Central Boulevard [7 A8]
CLIENT Midrand Town Council
STRUCTURAL ENGINEER BKS Structural Engineers
CONTRACT VALUE R5 million
GETTING THERE take the M1 highway north. At the Allandale/Grand Central Airport off-ramp, turn right. Cross over the M1, travel 0.7 kilometres and then turn left on to R101. After 4.7 kilometres, turn right into Grand Central Airport. Proceed a further 1.5 kilometres
ACCESS open

GAPP Architects & Urban Designers 1996

Midrand

GAPP Architects & Urban Designers 1996

Soweto

Soweto station upgrades

Prior to the 1994 elections, railway stations in South Africa were sites of extreme violence. The horrifying levels of violence galvanised Intersite, the development arm of the Rail Commuter Corporation, to appoint TPC Architects and a number of other consultants to try to address the issue of security and create more pleasant environments. The result was a flexible, instantly recognisable system building that could be erected while stations remained in operation – in short, a new image.

The strategy applied to the various stations follows a courtyard format with the station area itself, enclosed by walls or shops, offering some semblance of security. The main component is a structural steel frame incorporating a variety of shops; these are all small sheltered stands with roller-shutters on their frontages. The precinct around each station is defined by columns which form flagpoles along the perimeter while providing covered areas and walkways within. Entrance to the stations is through the shops, with a market area for hawkers outside.

The success of the scheme is hard to evaluate: the shopping areas have not done as well as had been hoped because the attraction of a rent-free spot just around the corner is hard to compete with. Incidences of violence have gone down, but that might simply be because there has been a change of government. The scheme's success lies perhaps in the inclusive process of implementation, from engaging the community through public awareness and participation programmes to the use of local labour.

CLIENT South African Rail Commuter Corporation
STRUCTURAL ENGINEER Keeve Steyn Inc.
CONTRACT VALUE R36 million (total for the two-phase development)
SIZE 16 stations
ACCESS open

TPC Architects 1993–96

Soweto

TPC Architects 1993–96

Soweto Careers Centre

The Soweto Careers Centre was established in 1978 in response to the crisis in black education that resulted from the 1976 Soweto student uprising. Its activities focus primarily on youth empowerment through professional guidance and counselling, as well as meeting related needs in the community at large.

The principal design requirements for this complex (an addition to the centre's existing multi-purpose hall, classroom and computer block) was that it should be multifunctional, with a culturally neutral aesthetic. While conventional in plan, Noero's lean, industrial solution provides a fine display of thorough detailing and inventive design.

The complex is set at an oblique angle to the dusty main road through Soweto, fixed between the existing building along the back of the site and a triangular parking area in front. Buffered from the noise and pollution of the busy traffic, the complex turns inwards, adopting a valley section. Its peaks – light scoops to the hall and classroom block – appear as dramatic hooded protrusions from which side roofs slope to a protected central courtyard. Internally, this device (which also allows for natural ventilation) makes for fantastic spaces.

In the brightly coloured classrooms, the unusual light source is used to create an altar-like backdrop behind the lecturer or course leader. In the hall, the sweeping section soars from the intimate scale of the door height and is transformed into an ambiguous duo-pitch symmetry by a series of triangular fins. This change in relationship is expressed on the building's side elevation where one entire wall is designed to slide away, integrating the hall interior with its exterior courtyard space for special functions.

Throughout the complex the material and spatial interplay between inside/outside space seems effortlessly achieved. While the approach to

Jo Noero Architects 1992

Soweto

Jo Noero Architects 1992

materials reflects the relatively tight budget, their application conveys transparent architectural concept and construction – purpose and function are always clearly evident. Bold signage reinforces the legibility of place.

ADDRESS corner Old Potchefstroom Road and Immink Street [48 C4]
CLIENT Soweto Careers Centre Trust
STRUCTURAL ENGINEER Rosnovanu & Associates
CONTRACT VALUE R1 million
SIZE approximately 1000 square metres
GETTING THERE travel west on Old Potchefstroom Road (M68), past Baragwanath Hospital; turn right at the next set of traffic lights (at BP garage). Drive through the BP garage to the entrance of the centre
ACCESS open

Jo Noero Architects 1992

Soweto

Jo Noero Architects 1992

Funda Centre Community College

Like the neighbouring Soweto Careers Centre, also by Noero (see page 222), the Funda Centre has its origins in the 1976 Soweto student uprising. Established in 1984, the centre is committed to engaging the Soweto community in innovative educational and cultural development programmes. The two phases of this project, an administration building and lecture block, constitute additions to the centre's existing buildings by architect Leon van Schaik.

The two-storey drum of the administration centre appears as a free-standing pavilion and provides the focus for the surrounding buildings. A canopied entrance portico protrudes from the rusticated brick base which is cut at regular intervals by long slots of glazing. Topped with a roof terrace, the upper level is by contrast a lightweight steel frame structure articulated by fin-like sun-control screens.

Internal organisation is based on the overlapping geometries of the circular plan and the square central lightwell which contains a spiral staircase connecting the upper office/boardroom level with the lower level of open-plan offices and cellular archive and print rooms.

The generating principle for the adjacent lecture block is a square open-air court around which radiate a series of classrooms of varying sizes.

ADDRESS Immink Street [49 A6]
CLIENT Funda Centre
STRUCTURAL ENGINEER Makenzie Cairns & Browne
CONTRACT VALUE R2.9 million SIZE 2500 square metres
GETTING THERE travel west on Old Potchefstroom Road (M68). Pass Baragwanath Hospital; turn right at next traffic lights (at BP garage). The entrance is on your left, approximately 200 metres from the traffic lights
ACCESS open

Soweto

Jo Noero Architects 1995

Soweto

Jo Noero Architects 1995

Johannesburg, surrounding areas

Vaal Triangle Technikon grandstand

Erected on top of an existing clubhouse building, this grandstand provides a simple and elegant architectural solution to what was essentially an engineering problem. The addition is basically a trussed and tensioned steel structure accommodating seating for 2 500 spectators as well as VIP rooms, broadcast facilities, additional changing rooms and storage space. From afar it appears deceptively small; it is only as you approach that its scale becomes apparent.

The grandstand superstructure consists of 14 structural steel members each comprising a beam which supports the seating at a 30-degree angle; a vertical column integrated into the column structure of the existing building; and a truss which, tensioned back through the column, holds up the canopy. The structural clarity of the lightweight members is complemented by direct, uncluttered detailing. A blue and postbox red colour scheme contrasts with the yellow facebrick walls of the clubhouse. New and old have been so well integrated that it is hard to tell them apart.

It is a steep climb to the top of the grandstand, but all the seating gives clear and unobstructed views of events.

ADDRESS at the corner of Barrage Road and Andries Potgieter Boulevard, Vanderbijlpark
CLIENT Vaal Triangle Technikon
STRUCTURAL ENGINEER Christo van der Merwe & Partners
CONTRACT VALUE R2 million
GETTING THERE take the R59 south to Vanderbijlpark. Then take the Vanderbijlpark off-ramp; this becomes Barrage Road
ACCESS open

Geldenhuys & Jooste 1995

Johannesburg, surrounding areas

Geldenhuys & Jooste 1995

Ivy Villa stables and studio

For this project, the architect-as-client scenario provided the vehicle for a rule-challenging personal statement. The house (the 'stables') and studio occupy a portion of the subdivided property of Ivy Villa, an Edwardian residence to which the house once served as an outbuilding. Conceived of as follies, the two separate but related buildings are set within a distorted checkerboard of gravel, plant and pond. The garden's skewed grid is a reference to the framed twist of Pretoria's city grid and provides the basis for the buildings' conflicting geometries.

A brick wall bisecting the site diagonally forms the portal between public and private domains. Annexed from the house, the studio stands exposed to the street, fixed between the wall and its intersecting pathway. Its design is a whimsical reinterpretation of the utilitarian, corrugated iron-shed structure of the house. Characterised by uncluttered assembly, architectural elements are isolated as independent entities. The most striking feature is a glazed inverted roof which, breezily thumbing its nose at convention, relates explicitly to the pitched roof of the existing building. Clip-on glass bays, large windows and a sequence of patios give the compact interiors a sense of spaciousness.

ADDRESS 41 Ivy Street, Clydesdale, Pretoria CLIENT Ora Joubert STRUCTURAL ENGINEER Gerrit Lombard RETICULATION Marnus Barnard CONTRACT VALUE R160,000 SIZE 160 square metres (house and studio) GETTING THERE take the Pietersburg Highway (N1) to Pretoria; take the Lynnwood turn-off and turn right into Kirkness Street. Proceed past Loftus (rugby stadium) and turn left into Faranden Street. Turn right at the end of Villa Street and proceed; the complex is at the corner of Villa and Ivy Streets
ACCESS by appointment (telephone Ora Joubert on 012 344 3454)

Ora Joubert 1995

Ora Joubert 1995

Group housing

One cannot imagine this as a European or Californian house – it is an unmistakably South African solution that is appropriate to the climate. The first in a proposed three-unit housing development, its dominant feature is a thatched roof, which continues the theme set by the original house by Helmut Stauch in the 1950s.

Here Joubert has created a synthesis between the vernacular and Corbusian model: the expansive thatched roof and its blue gum pole supporting structure establish an independent enclosure allowing total flexibility in the articulation of free-standing internal walls. Inside, one experiences the double volumes and thatched roof from every vantage point and, through the system of geometric pavilions, varying qualities of openness and privacy.

A cut back to the pitch on the north side allows the pavilions to extend beyond the roof line, lifting the skirt of the roof so that light penetrates generously into the first-floor areas and into the depth of the house at its lower levels. The interior is characterised by tactile finishes: large glass areas fixed with silicon, and massive, richly coloured wall panels that superbly complement the rustic primary structure.

ADDRESS 341 Brooklyn Road, Pretoria
CLIENT Cornelius Laubscher STRUCTURAL ENGINEER Gerrit Lombard
CONTRACT VALUE R450,000 SIZE 180 square metres
GETTING THERE take the Pietersburg Highway (N1) to Pretoria. Take the Lynnwood turn off; proceed along Lynnwood Road and then turn left into Brooklyn Road. The house is at the second set of traffic lights, on the corner of Charles and Brooklyn Roads1
ACCESS by appointment (telephone Cornelius Laubscher on 083 626 7605)

Ora Joubert 1997

Johannesburg, surrounding areas

Ora Joubert 1997

Makalali game reserve

When the Conservation Corporation and the entrepreneur Charles Smith bought 10,000 hectares of cattle-farming land on the gravelotte road between Phalaborwa and Hoedspruit with the aim of turning it into a game reserve, the restocking and regeneration of the veld was a priority. With this came the desire to build a game lodge with a difference.

Bush camp or lost city? On the banks of the Makhutsi River in Mpumalanga, Silvio Rech has side-stepped the clichés to create a new kind of African adventure. Out of the fabric of the landscape – rock, trees, red sand and grass – a series of fantastical buildings has crystallised. Above the river bank, a ripple of thatch and clay raised on stilts and tipped with shining horns has been woven through the trees.

The project used the creative skills of the workforce involved to shape the building, with the development of the designs largely carried out on site. What has emerged is a marvellously inventive environment in which every detail, from taps to latches to candleholders, has been reinvented. Expect Indiana Jones!

ADDRESS Makalali (between Phalaborwa and Hoedspruit), Mpumalanga
CLIENTS Charles Smith, The Conservation Corporation
GETTING THERE by air from Johannesburg to Phalabowa airport
ACCESS by appointment (telephone the Conservation Corporation on 011 784 6832)

Silvio Rech 1996

Silvio Rech 1996

Central Durban

Mansel Road Development

In inner-city Durban more than in any other South African city, people living and trading on the pavement are a familiar sight. Here, the street is home to more than 3000 people.

This project was primarily initiated because of the Newmarket Street Squatters, who used to live in shacks lining both sides of Newmarket Street between First Avenue and Mitchel Crescent near the Greyville racecourse, selling their bulky water drums to the passengers of long-distance buses stopping nearby. The squatters' presence, legitimised with the change of government, blocked what was potentially a massive housing scheme. To get them off the site, the city offered them housing on an adjoining piece of vacant land – a 'win-win' situation for all involved. The result is the first formal attempt in recent South Africa to bring the poor back into the 'apartheid city'.

The development is on a long strip of land left over when the railway lines were realigned after the train station was moved out of the Central Business District. The new building provides the traders with homes in the form of a 'wall' of units along the railway line, with a bus parking area in front.

The units are very basic. The single-room front layer of the building provides a shop outlet with a high frontage for advertising and a tip-up panel opening to a sales counter. This is divided from the sleeping/living room to the rear by a courtyard covered with a pergola – the idea being that residents can cover the yard with tarpaulin or plastic if they want to increase the size of their living area. These courtyards also provide play areas for children, or they can be converted for small business ventures such as overnight lodgings.

Buses cruise in and out via access points at either end of the 'street'. Because the buses come from considerable distances (often more than

Harber Masson Associates 1996

Central Durban

Harber Masson Associates 1996

1000 kilometres), a key requirement of the brief was the provision of bathing and sleeping facilities for the bus drivers. Offering the street people of Durban 20 litres of solar-heated water for a nominal cost, this 'Roman baths' building is the pivotal structure, located at the head of the complex. The entrance is marked by a triangular tower which provides important security for the representatives of rural villages who often arrive carrying large sums of money to purchase goods for the people at home.

The scheme has developed to encompass a covered market area and approximately 200 parking bays where car-boot sellers trade at night.

ADDRESS Mansel Road [26 B3]
CLIENT City of Durban
STRUCTURAL ENGINEER Orator & Associates/Michael Noyce
CONTRACT VALUE R9.6 million
SIZE 220 square metres (public baths), 2500 square metres (housing units x 44), 2100 square metres (car-boot sales), 3250 square metres (short-term accommodation)
GETTING THERE off Umgeni Road
ACCESS open

Harber Masson Associates 1996

Harber Masson Associates 1996

Warwick Avenue Bridge Market

The site of this market is the commuter centre of Durban, where buses and taxis – both public and entrepreneurial – and trains converge from the north, south and west. An interchange node with an energy born from the legitimisation of informal economic pursuit, this is a place with the vibrancy of a new African city. It is also the *real* city centre – Durban's urban heart of hawkers, shacks and shebeens (speakeasies) in an African Bladerunner setting.

Alongside the city's principal train station a truncated flyover, going nowhere, is now the site of an urban event: a 9-metre-high pedestrian bridge where traders ply their wares. The lightweight steel structure stretches between the concrete masses of the existing footbridge to the station and the unfinished highway. On the flyover's buttressed end, an 8-metre-high mural of the African goddess Nomkubulwa, Mama Africa, awaits, her arms outstretched in a gesture of greeting and protection.

The bridge has an independent character, its negative building form contrasting with the solidity of its anchors. Mid-crossing, its basic form mutates to accommodate trading along its length, with the main bridge trusses developing outriggers which support extended trading areas on either side of the main aisle. Entrance at either end is marked by a supporting structure resembling flat crown trees, its freeform canopies are sheltering clouds of *izintingu* (wattle branches used in vernacular African construction). It has a transient quality that reflects the natural dynamics of trading patterns.

The unfinished highway is the site of a formal building – initially single storey but with extension to a double-storey structure planned – housing the consulting rooms of the *nyangas* (traditional doctors). All along the unfinished highway are shelters for traditional herb traders, consisting of a roof, provision of electricity and water supply. The scheme reinforces

Design Workshop 1997

Design Workshop 1997

the infrastructural connection between the early morning market, the rail station, the principal bus terminus and the formal city centre, and together with the pavement below forms part of a seemingly endless, amorphous shopping centre.

Central Durban

ADDRESS Warwick Avenue [26 B1]
CLIENT City of Durban
STRUCTURAL ENGINEER Young & Satharia
CONTRACT VALUE R2.5 million
SIZE 1650 square metres (covered trading area); 150 metres square (*nyangas*' consulting rooms)
ACCESS open

Design Workshop 1997

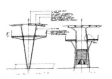 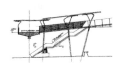

Design Workshop 1997

Victoria Street bus terminus

The reconstruction of the existing Victoria Street bus terminus provided for passenger, driver and security facilities co-ordinated with a new footbridge linked directly to the adjacent railway station. The triangular site is below two sections of elevated highway which bring high volumes of traffic into and out of the city. Since the roof level was to be virtually that of the raised freeway carriages, the view from the top of the building was an important consideration.

The design exploits and develops the structural properties of cranked corrugated sheet, vaulting to create an interesting roofscape that is virtually self-cleansing, terminating smoothly against the diverging curves of the freeways which bisect the site at either end. The structure's diagonal planning grid was determined by the access routes of the buses.

During the apartheid era, the elevated signboard/catwalk that draws out of the building allowed the security forces to secure the area completely. With the advent of the new South Africa, the terminus has attracted dozens of informal traders who live and sell beneath their plastic sheeted stalls on the surrounding pavements, making this a trading and transport hub.

Central Durban

ADDRESS junction of Alice Street and Market Road [26 B I]
CLIENT Durban Corporation (City Engineers' Department)
STRUCTURAL ENGINEER De Leuw Cather (partner in charge Pat Duffy)
SIZE 30 bays accommodating four buses each (provision for 6000 peak-hour passengers)
GETTING THERE take the western exit from Durban on to Berea Road
ACCESS open

Myles Pugh Sherlock Murray 1986

Myles Pugh Sherlock Murray 1986

Soldiers Way taxi rank

Ubiquitous symbols of successful black enterprise, minibus taxis provide millions of commuters with reasonably priced transport every day and give a degree of public accessibility to areas not serviced by buses. This fiercely competitive industry has developed at a phenomenal rate, often leaving facilities for taxis and commuters woefully inadequate. The creation of areas for these taxis to load and off-load passengers safely has been a priority in the city. In this case, in addition to a formal rank, the architects were asked to provide a roof as well as wash areas and facilities for the informal traders who inevitably gather around taxi ranks.

The result is this economical, functional yet elegant solution. Located on a highly visible island site, the rank's wave sequence of curved roofs provides a gateway to the city from the north. Supporting steel posts punching through the roof at its edges give the structure a sense of prominence, while its level canopy and the almost column-free space below allow for clear views across the rank to the city and Berea Ridge beyond.

Because of the need to retain flexibility for future development, the structure was designed to enable dismantling and relocation if necessary. Structural elements are simplified and junctions accentuated with bold, careful detailing. Today the design has become synonymous with the minibus taxi industry.

ADDRESS Soldiers Way [26 B3]
PROJECT ARCHITECT Gavin Adams
CLIENT City of Durban
STRUCTURAL ENGINEER De Leuw Cather in association with Vawda Thornton
CONTRACT VALUE R1.8 million
SIZE 3921 square metres (roof area) ACCESS open

Central Durban

Durban Architectural Services 1995

Durban Architectural Services 1995

Durban Water & Waste

Located at the edge of the Centrum (a 28-hectare tract of land made available for development when the railway authorities vacated their city-centre site in the 1970s), this building occupies a site bounded by roads on three sides. Its western edge fronts a public square which is defined by the KwaMuhle Museum and which terminates a pedestrian axis beginning at the City Hall. Given this context, the architects remodelled the square as a small-scale civic piazza with the building articulated to address both the civic and urban demands of the site. The result visibly strains to meet its responsibilities.

Its internal organisation is rational enough: two parallel wings containing a light-filled central court provide a comfortable working environment. Its exterior, however, presents a bewildering array of elements. The sides and rear of the five-storey building are layered with a two-storey red facebrick base in acknowledgement of the scale of the surrounding streetscape, and a verandah-like oversailing roof. The main façade on to the square is intended as a populist statement, a response to the client's expressed desire for a 'consumer-friendly' architecture. Here, a cascading water feature takes over. The entrance is marked by a steel canopy above which a waterdrum-like cylinder protrudes through the façade. Going overboard with the water associations, the extensive fenestration is of the nasty reflecting blue-tinted variety. The façade is overlaid rather arbitrarily by a gridded screen – more waste than water.

ADDRESS 3 Prior Road (off Ordnance Road) [26 B4]
CLIENT Durban Water & Waste Service Unit
STRUCTURAL ENGINEER Young & Satharia
CONTRACT VALUE R17 million SIZE 7000 square metres
ACCESS during office hours

Johnson Murray Architects 1994

Johnson Murray Architects 1994

Durban Health & Racquet Club

This building brought to an end a conservation battle that had been waged over this site since the early 1970s, when the railway stopped coming into the city centre. Formerly the old train shed, it is part of an ensemble of railway buildings which also includes the two old station workshops (now redeveloped as the Workshop Shopping Centre and Durban Exhibition Centre).

Its internal volume preserved, the building has found a new lease of life as the Durban Health & Racquet Club – a fitness mecca for the city's terminally trendy. Inside, the Victorian ironwork of its enclosing volume serves as the backdrop to the gym structure, which is essentially an insertion, structurally and visually independent from the old. While creating the dynamic spatial relationships that are de rigueur in a fashionably frenetic establishment such as this, the intervention nevertheless has a remarkably low-key presence which succeeds in reinforcing the character of the original.

Externally the building maintains its Victorian utilitarian character, standing in relative isolation as it awaits integration with the Centrum (see page 252) via Locomotive Plaza. Its surrounding parking lot occupies the site once earmarked for the museum component of Uytenbogaardt and Rozendal's 1989 competition-winning Cultural Centre.

ADDRESS 2 Soldiers Way [26 B3]
CLIENT Durban Health & Racquet Club
STRUCTURAL ENGINEER Keeve Steyn Inc.
CONTRACT VALUE R8 million
SIZE 4000 square metres
ACCESS it is usually possible to look around – announce yourself

Johnson Murray Architects 1995

Central Durban

Johnson Murray Architects 1995

Central Durban

International Convention Centre

Durban has been debating the merits of a convention centre for at least two decades. With South Africa's acceptance into the international community, the long-held dream has become a reality. This centre is seen as the catalyst for local economic development, bringing the city into contact with international markets.

A requirement of the brief was that an 'international' architect should be engaged to assist with the scheme's initial zoning. After contact with such luminaries as Terry Farrell and Michael Wilfred, the architects appointed Sydney-based Philip Cox – who had been involved in four similar projects – to lend his expertise.

On the site of the old Central Prison, the centre lies adjacent to the Centrum (see page 252), for which the architects provided an urban design framework. Essentially, the area was to be a pedestrian precinct, its periphery walled by buildings which would provide for various formal and informal activities while at the same time shielding it from the surrounding traffic. This 'people's plaza' would be linked to rest of the city via pedestrian routes.

The Convention Centre is positioned on the northern portion of its site, allowing for future expansion to the south, and with an associated hotel (the Durban Hilton, see page 260) located on a bulge at the north-west corner of the site.

Like its neighbour, the Durban Exhibition Centre, the building is essentially a large volume (160 x 50 x 10 metres) to which some smaller-scale elements are attached. The simple, linear form accommodates a glazed triple-volume entrance foyer at its fulcrum; a plenary hall with hinged seating which can be used either as a flat-floor venue or a normal raked auditorium; and two other halls offering flexible configurations. A concourse along the western side acts as the principal circulation spine,

Stauch Vorster Architects 1997

Stauch Vorster Architects 1997

giving access to the various halls and some smaller meeting rooms set away from the main building. These are bordered by planted courtyards designed to provide outside venues for local functions.

The centre's most striking external feature is its expansive undulating roof – a lightweight construction of aluminium sheeting on steel trusses from which verandah-like extensions draw out on three sides of the building (the rather inelegant, blunt southern end awaits future extension). Brought down low over pedestrian areas, the wavy canopy adds a sensual, organic quality to the building, appearing like a giant, hovering manta ray. On the eastern (service) side of the building, the overhangs remain relatively high, sheltering loading bays.

The centre will undoubtedly prove an asset to the city and its people. It seems a pity, however, that it does not include the public facilities that would ensure a life beyond the big events, although its use programme attempts to accommodate this need.

This is a building in which exemplary design skills are evident in the disciplined integration of concept, ordering principles and details.

ADDRESS Ordnance Road [26 B4]
CLIENT ICC Construction (Pty) Ltd
ASSOCIATE ARCHITECTS Hallen Custers Smith and Johnson Murray Architects
CONSULTING ARCHITECT Philip Cox
STRUCTURAL ENGINEER Lawrence & Boorsma in association with Young & Satharia
CONTRACT VALUE R200 million
SIZE 28,000 square metres (excluding parking)
ACCESS limited

Central Durban

Stauch Vorster Architects 1997

Stauch Vorster Architects 1997

Durban Hilton

The Durban Hilton represents the international hotel chain's first foray into South Africa. Adjacent to the city's new International Convention Centre (see page 256), it was designed to cater primarily for business and convention clients.

The form of the building is a response to the restricted site. It picks up the dynamics of the Convention Centre with soft lines and a wave form reflecting its proximity to the sea. Covering the entire site, the hotel presents a hard exterior to two roads. Bars and restaurants open on to terraces, forming an interface with the Convention Centre. These public areas open off a triple-volume atrium, while the major external space is in the form of a roof terrace on the second-floor level.

The soft lines continue into the bedroom tower, which has 12 standard floors terminating in a series of stepped terraces. External finishes are of a high quality, with granite and sandstone at podium level giving way to aluminium and glass on the upper levels. The use of stainless steel adds sparkle and contrast to the natural stone finishes, while the light reflecting off the curved façade gives the tower an ever-changing face.

Artwork is an integral part of the design; canopies and architectural features are as much pieces of sculpture as part of the building.

ADDRESS 61 Ordnance Road (Walnut Road entrance) [26 B4]
CLIENT Renong Overseas Corporation
STRUCTURAL ENGINEER Africon Consulting Engineers
GLASS MANUFACTURER PFG Building Glass (Pty) Ltd
CONTRACT VALUE R215 million
SIZE 34,664 square metres (including parking)
ACCESS by appointment (contact John Lovell on 031 336 8100)

Central Durban

FGG Architects 1997

Central Durban

FGG Architects 1997

88 Field Street

As with Johannesburg's 11 Diagonal Street (see page 138), the client/architect combination of Anglo American Properties and Chicago-based practice Murphy/Jahn spawned an instant landmark with this dramatic retail and office complex. A shimmering reflection of sky and surrounding buildings, 88 Field Street is visible from virtually every corner of the city.

At street level, the complex provides shops along a through-block arcade, continuing a city tradition. Its contextual appropriateness ends right there – the 24-storey office tower above is pure Chicago glitz. Its appearance is a sculptural expression of two concentric octagons spiralling to the heavens. As it corkscrews it steps to provide a planted roof terrace at each office level – a small concession to Durban's subtropical climate. Its defiant culmination is a bold crow's-nest pinnacle and spire.

Before it was built in Durban, the design had a dry-run as a competition entry for an office block in Kentucky, US. In reconciling the original vision with the new context, the recycled design presents some intriguing contradictions: for example, where steel construction would be expected, prefabricated concrete has been used. The adept handling of the building's upper storeys gives way to some clumsy moves at street level. Canopied edges along side streets perversely disappear at the main entrance where a mundane little 'greenhouse' protrusion provides access to the arcade.

Central Durban

ADDRESS 88 Field Street [26 B3]
ASSOCIATE ARCHITECT Stauch Vorster Architects
CLIENT Anglo American Properties
STRUCTURAL ENGINEER Ove Arup & Partners
SIZE 24,500 square metres
ACCESS open at ground level; limited access to office levels

Murphy/Jahn 1986

Murphy/Jahn 1986

Metropolitan Life Building

In the heart of the CBD, this project started – literally – with a bang, since the building previously occupying part of its site was demolished in Durban's first ever implosion.

Bounded by narrow side streets, the 16-storey tower stands proudly independent of its neighbours on half a city block. Its design exploits this isolation, making a grand gesture on the main Smith Street façade, which is characterised by a bowed curtain wall framed on either side by quadrant corners. A classical division to the frontage distinguishes a capital through balcony recesses to the top office floors where the quadrants become three-quarter-drum office suites. A two-dimensionally curved pediment forms its crown. Steel constructions provide a feature in the form of 'Lady Liberty' terminations to the top and bottom of the quadrants and a halo-like canopy at the base. The base is a heavy, granite-clad podium, accommodating retail and parking space, into which a red cubic frame juts obliquely to signal the foyer entrance.

Exterior finishes consist of silver, grey and African red contrasting horizontal bands. The exuberance of the main elevation gives way to mediocrity on the side elevations which are bland, standard spec office fare.

ADDRESS 393 Smith Street [26 C3]
CLIENT Esplanbea (Pty) Ltd (subsidiary of Metropolitan Life Ltd)
ASSOCIATE ARCHITECT Dirksen Blumenfeld & Krause
STRUCTURAL ENGINEERS L S C Brunette & Partners (Durban) and Partnership De Villiers (Cape)
CONTRACT VALUE R50 million
SIZE 12,000 square metres
ACCESS 8.00–16.30

Central Durban

Stafford Associate Architects 1994

Stafford Associate Architects 1994

Investec Bank

This project involved the conservation and substantial enlargement of the former Reserve Bank (W G Moffat & Hirst, 1935–39). Modelled on its Johannesburg counterpart (designed by Gordon Leith), the building is an important example of the Union Classical style. Because of its rich granite and sandstone construction and the exquisite resolution of its composition, additions had to be subtle and discreet. A sensitive treatment was achieved thanks to the client giving up valuable space and the architects deferring to the character of the existing building.

The extension – a roof addition and rear wing – is respectfully subservient to the original architecture. The roof addition is set back from the street, concealed from passers-by, while the addition to the rear has a low-key modern character which recedes self-deprecatingly from the streetline where it appears as a thin, planar object behind the solid mass of the bank. Internally, the three-storey addition is composed around an atrium which is skylit at the top to filter sunlight into the existing oculi of the domes above the ground-level banking hall. The new spaces provide a pleasant, light-filled working environment, interspersed with planters, giving access to a roof terrace.

ADDRESS 325 Smith Street [26 B4]
CLIENT Investec Bank
ASSOCIATE ARCHITECT Stafford Associate Architects
STRUCTURAL ENGINEER Kampel Abramowitz Yawitch & Partners
CONTRACT VALUE R10 million
SIZE 6000 square metres
ACCESS none

Central Durban

Kosseff van der Walt Architects 1995

Kosseff van der Walt Architects 1995

Old Mutual Centre

This, the tallest building in central Durban, stands on what is arguably the city's most important piece of real estate – the western half of the historic Farewell Square (a civic space fronted by the Post Office and City Hall), reaching from Gardiner Street to Mercury Lane. Consequently, the evolution of an urban design strategy for the whole site was an important consideration in Stauch Vorster's scheme, entailing the completion of landscaping already surrounding three sides of the square and the creation of a promenade relationship to the street.

The Old Mutual Centre itself follows a tower-on-podium format with ground-level retail space and parking above. Rather than presenting the usual bland façade, the parking levels are partially lined by offices clad externally in sandstone in acknowledgement of the historic buildings nearby. A flared segmented arch marks the entrance, announced by a pavement recess, a giant portal and two clusters of palm trees.

As with Old Mutual Properties' Safmarine House development (see page 30) where a cruciform-type arrangement was applied, here an X-shaped core plan provides perimeter offices in corner projections, maximising views. These are differentiated from the core by the window treatment and by different coloured cladding. The effect is of a ponderous tower element which sits uneasily on its base. The building's dominance of the square is a result of its sheer bulk rather than any iconic quality.

ADDRESS 323 West Street (corner of Mercury Lane) [26 B4]
ASSOCIATE ARCHITECT Interarc
CLIENT Old Mutual Properties
STRUCTURAL ENGINEER Kampel Abramowitz Yawitch & Partners
CONTRACT VALUE R150 million SIZE 32,000 square metres
ACCESS open

Stauch Vorster Architects 1996

Stauch Vorster Architects 1996

50 Prince Alfred Street refurbishment

On the periphery of Durban's light-industrial area, this little gem is a strikingly refreshing apparition in a very drab urban landscape. The architects were commissioned to refurbish an existing building and create a new open entrance and reception area in keeping with the dynamic image of the client, a growing shipping company.

The existing building, a facebrick international-style design with numerous plastered horizontal ledges, has been 'smoothed out' and 'modernised'. The nature of the brief ensured that this was to be largely an exercise in façadism and decorative architecture. The exception is the 'prow' of the reception area which steams up the confluence of Prince Alfred Street and Commercial Road. Its western façade, funked up with slatted sun-control screens and an extroverted entrance foyer, takes full advantage of its corner siting.

Materials and details were selected to reflect the nature of the primary occupant, the shipping company, while at the same time projecting a machine-like image of up-to-date efficiency.

ADDRESS 50 Prince Alfred Street [26 B4]
CLIENT Panafco Maritime/Tora Investments
STRUCTURAL ENGINEER Oldfield Roberts & Associates
PROJECT TEAM Dean Jay, Paul Nel, Luke Scott, Stuart Maclaughlan and Thomas Steer
CONTRACT VALUE R700,000
SIZE 1600 square metres (existing building), 50 square metres (newly built area)
ACCESS reception area open during normal office hours

Central Durban

Dean Jay Architects 1996

Dean Jay Architects 1996

Ocean Terminal refurbishment

Designed in 1960, the Ocean Terminal building epitomised the Brasilia style common to many of South Africa's public projects of the period. With the demise of mail-ship operations, it fell into disuse and became something of a white elephant on Durban's harbour.

Bringing the terminal building a new lease of life, this refurbishment was designed to house the offices of Portnet, a company created by the restructuring of South African Railways and Harbours. Previously scattered across several sites around the city, Portnet's 300 staff now occupy the building's old customs hall – a vast space, nine metres high. This is accessed via the original arrivals hall to which a new entrance has been added. A double-volume internal street framed by mezzanine levels forms the main circulation route. As it gently contracts and expands following a curve along its western edge, this canyon-like space reveals a range of vistas. The detailing creates a nautical aesthetic – hardwood salvaged from old customs counters and baggage racks is used for decking and stair treads while turnbuckles and stainless-steel cables provide the balustrading. Blue castellated steel I-beams constitute the primary supporting members which contrast strongly with the robust original structure.

ADDRESS Ocean Terminal Building, Durban Harbour [26 4D]
PROJECT ARCHITECT David Stromberg
CLIENT Portnet
STRUCTURAL ENGINEER ZAI (Natal) Inc.
CONTRACT VALUE R10 million
SIZE 5500 square metres
GETTING THERE via Stanger Street port entrance off Victoria Embankment
ACCESS open office hours – announce yourself at reception

Central Durban

Protekon 1993

Protekon 1993

136 Victoria Embankment

The site was a challenging one: a slither measuring 12 x 70 metres squeezed between two street junctions edging the Bay of Natal and subject to three different zoning regulations. Rising to the occasion, Interarc produced a functional office building whose powerful presence embodies the spirit of the Victoria Embankment.

The building's framework is effectively shaped by its site constraints. To enable efficient circulation on the upper levels, the entrance is positioned along a side street between a retail component at the front of the building and parking to the rear. The success of the design is the main façade. Split into two, it takes its cue from the imaginative corner treatments that are characteristic of the Victoria Embankment. A tight glass skin following the curve at the front of the site peels away to reveal a stack of jagged, stepped balconies which have stunning views over the bay and waterfront. The façade division is reconciled by a segment-vaulted hood which is in fact the jutting penthouse roof of a private penthouse suite. The bay location and the owner's association with the yachting scene have inspired a nautical theme – windows become portholes, balustrades are ship's railings, and the front of the building resembles a prow.

Though dwarfed by its neighbours, this compact little building packs a mean punch.

ADDRESS 136 Victoria Embankment [26 C3]
CLIENT Safegro Property Management Ltd
STRUCTURAL ENGINEER L S C Brunette & Partners
CONTRACT VALUE R10 million
SIZE 5000 square metres
ACCESS public areas open during office hours

Central Durban

Interarc 1993

Interarc 1993

Café Fish waterfront restaurant

How do you deal with a site with no corner pegs? How do you finance a building with no title deeds? And how does the council approve a plan with no street address?

In their mission to make the harbour accessible to all the people of Durban rather than to just the members of a few exclusive clubs, Architects Collaborative managed to jump these and other bureaucratic hurdles. After protracted negotiations, permission was obtained from the port authorities to locate this restaurant adjacent to the bay services jetty in the yacht basin.

Taking its place among the masts and sails, the restaurant is a jolly, transparent, lightweight structure. A 'boat' built on stilts, it takes its cue from the colourful yachts around it.

Proposed major developments elsewhere in the harbour may incorporate other restaurants, so although this is seen as an interesting pilot project, it has been given only a relatively short lease. The architects have taken this into consideration, using innovative and cost-effective construction methods which will enable the client to demolish the building easily, if necessary, when the lease expires.

ADDRESS Yacht Mole [26 C3]
CLIENT Durban Waterfront Holdings
STRUCTURAL ENGINEER Lawrence & Boorsma
CONTRACT VALUE R1.6 million
SIZE 350 square metres
GETTING THERE take the bus to the Esplanade; cross the railway line from the Esplanade into Durban harbour and turn left
ACCESS open

Central Durban

Architects Collaborative 1995

Central Durban

Architects Collaborative 1995

The BAT Centre

The BAT Centre is in a tough environment, situated in the working harbour alongside the tug basin, with fantastic views over the bustle of the Bay of Natal. The result of the metamorphosis of an existing structure, the Navy's SAS Inkonkoni building, it is a private initiative of the Bartel Arts Trust, providing a unique forum for cross-cultural activities and events.

Nestled in its corner of the harbour, the centre seems to accept, to celebrate even, its difficult access route. In so doing, it turns its back on the city, directing its main façade towards the harbour. Two pavilions embrace a central section set behind a purple-blue painted balcony which oversails a colonnade. Behind the colonnade, a row of openings provides access to shops, a resource centre and a computer outlet. The upper level of the south pavilion houses administrative offices while the north pavilion contains Funky's Restaurant. With its services facing on to the city side, the main façade is covered in a tattoo of murals.

The structural concept of the building is inspired by the curved roof and bowstring trusses over the hall of the old Inkonkoni hall, once the enclosed core of the 'ship', now a performance venue. Instead of trusses, the skeleton is formed by a series of cross-walls at 5-metre centres which rise to different heights to pick up the telephone-pole purlins over which corrugated iron roofs are stretched. This simple and economical system ensures unity with the existing roof and creates an interesting roofscape for the building overlooking it. At entry level, the channel of spaces (the bar, a small gallery and a terrace facing on to the bay) links the wings of the building.

The BAT Centre is intended to be a model demonstrating that memorable buildings do not have to be excessive or expensive, and that one can use cheap, simple, often recycled materials without affecting the

Architects Collaborative 1995

Central Durban

Architects Collaborative 1995

quality of the experience. Providing a sound focus for the new, integrating South Africa, the centre represents and accommodates a fresh heterogeneity.

Central Durban

ADDRESS Maritime Place, Durban Harbour [26 C4]
CLIENT Bartel Arts Trust
STRUCTURAL ENGINEER Young & Satharia
CONTRACT VALUE R2.3 million (equipped)
SIZE 3400 square metres
GETTING THERE bus to the Esplanade; cross the railway line from the Esplanade into Durban harbour and turn left. Proceed for 700 metres
ACCESS open (ask at the administration offices for a tour)

Architects Collaborative 1995

Architects Collaborative 1995

Durban, The Ridge

59 Musgrave Road

Formerly the architects' own offices and studio, this glass addition is an extension to one of Musgrave Road's oldest buildings, a Victorian villa known as 'Monaltrie', originally built in 1897. The design of the new addition is a ghostly echo of the original architecture – a contemporary expression creating a harmonious yet distinct backdrop. Form and materials highlight the contrast between old and new, providing a balanced composition in which the distinctive elements of the sheltering verandah and gables are reinterpreted and reconfigured, albeit a little more two-dimensionally than in the Victorian anchor.

The connection to the existing building respects the separateness of the two structures by a setback and the asymmetrical positioning of the addition. Spatially, the link is used for circulation to the various levels and forms a bridge between the old and new sections.

Concerns of contextual appropriateness go beyond the mere mimicking of existing details. This is an attempt to catch the spirit of the past within an appropriate architecture of today.

Durban, The Ridge

ADDRESS 59 Musgrave Road, Morningside [20 D2]
CLIENT Stauch Vorster Architects
STRUCTURAL ENGINEER Lawrence & Boorsma
CONTRACT VALUE R1.5 million
SIZE 1000 square metres
ACCESS exterior access only

Stauch Vorster Architects 1987

Stauch Vorster Architects 1987

KNSA Gallery

The Kwazulu-Natal Society of Arts' decision to hold a local competition for its new gallery, and the successful completion of this winning proposal, provided advocates of the competition system with some much needed support.

The winning entry was by Walters & Cohen who have offices in London as well as Durban. Their design is a sophisticated and clear resolution to the brief, which called for a gallery space, two workshop areas, a crafts shop, restaurant facilities, an office and a tea garden.

On the edge of Bulwer Park, the site stands in the trendy suburb of Glenwood, next to a modest Victorian building housing the regional architects' institute. The building takes the form of two interlocking rectangles. The solid form, built of bagged hollow concrete block, contains utility spaces. By contrast, the circulation and gallery are enclosed in a light steel-frame envelope of glass and wooden slatted screens, skewed in plan to accentuate the perspective of the entrance ambulatory, providing a stepped auditorium-like space for exhibition openings.

The brick-finished staircase tapers upwards to a secondary entrance off Bath Road and via the workshop to a mezzanine level inside. The façade looking on to the garden space is constructed from slatted iroko screens in a steel framework; these tip up to provide access to the stairs at both the upper and lower ends of the gallery and allow a constant flow of air into the building, keeping it wonderfully cool even in Durban's hot, humid climate.

As a result of the tight budget, finishes are unabashedly rough, with fastidious finishes reserved for tactile areas such as shop shelving, balustrading and handles. The use of U and H sections to support the gently sloping corrugated-iron roof and recessed guttering gives the building a Miesian refinement. This is an unashamedly contemporary building.

Durban, The Ridge

Walters & Cohen 1996

Durban, The Ridge

Walters & Cohen 1996

Although the building has come in for some criticism because of its lack of enclosure, the direct sunlight on the main display wall, and some circulation problems, as a gallery it provides an uncluttered and spacious background for the display of art. Function and form are evident and clear. The juxtaposition of solid and void is not an new concept, but here it has been executed with astonishing elegance and simplicity.

Durban, The Ridge

ADDRESS 166 Bulwer Road, Glenwood [25 C8]
CLIENT Kwazulu-Natal Society of Arts
STRUCTURAL ENGINEER Young & Satharia
CONTRACT VALUE R1.3 million
SIZE 800 square metres
GETTING THERE Mynah bus to Davenport Road
ACCESS open Tuesday to Friday 9.00–17.00, Saturday 9.00–16.00, Sunday 10.00–15.00, closed Monday

Walters & Cohen 1996

Walters & Cohen 1996

Costa Maningi offices

The residential suburb of Glenwood provides the fashionably decentralised location for these offices for a firm of consulting engineers. This compact linear building occupies a long narrow site which is part of an area rezoned for commercial use.

Externally, the building is characterised by a playful though confident 'Legoland' approach: the strongly geometric entrance façade appears as a grey tiled cube out of which openings have been punctured; two concrete beams painted a deep terracotta cantilever over the cube. The length of the building is punctuated by small windows exaggerated by a low plaster relief. A curved roof set above a band of clerestory glazing extends over the entrance, its turquoise steelwork exposed.

The slight fall of the land allows for an entrance foyer at half level, providing access to ground and first floors. The double-volume drawing office on the lower level relates spatially and visually to a gallery on the upper floor – a communication thoroughfare giving access to the boardroom and open-plan offices on the upper level. The curve of the roof is echoed internally by the gently barrelled acoustic tile ceiling concealing the turquoise steelwork left exposed outside.

ADDRESS 28 Devonshire Avenue, Glenwood [26 CI]
DESIGN ARCHITECT Barbara van Zyl
CLIENT Delen & Oudkerk
STRUCTURAL ENGINEER Horne Glasson & Partners
SIZE 270 square metres
GETTING THERE Mynah bus to Glenwood (bus stop corner Devonshire Avenue and Davenport Road)
ACCESS open during business hours

Durban, The Ridge

FGG Architects 1991

FGG Architects 1991

Innovation Centre, Foundation Offices and Law Centre

The Innovation Centre is a new concept at the University of Natal. Conceived of as the interface between the rarefied environment of academe and the world outside, it is intended to provide a framework within which the university can serve the broader community through a wide range of skills-enhancement programmes.

This building, set on rugged terrain west of the university's main campus, forms the first component of the Innovation Centre masterplan and houses several independent units as well as communal facilities – a library, lecture theatre and cafeteria – planned for the use of the centre as a whole. Poised to receive future additions, the building nonetheless appears complete and self-contained.

The main entrance is skewed off the building's south-east corner, penetrating its protective exterior to lead directly into a tranquil, rectangular inner court. Reminiscent of a monastic cloister, this inner court provides the centre's organisational core. Its sides contain a framework of cellular offices to which large seminar rooms, set at a 45-degree angle to the façade, create recessed entry points. Communal facilities are expressed as distinct geometric volumes at opposing ends of the courtyard – the library takes the form of a cube at the entrance, while a circular drum-shaped lecture theatre closes the space at the far end.

Designed as a separate structure, the lecture theatre drum with the cafeteria on its lower level forms the node on to which successive phases of the centre will be developed. With the enclosed blind box of the lecture theatre suspended within the void of the cafeteria below, the two parts are locked in an interplay of mass and void. They are linked via dual stairways which, embracing the insertion, lead from the cafeteria to the theatre foyer at courtyard level.

Durban, The Ridge

Hallen Custers Smith 1993

Hallen Custers Smith 1993

The success of the design lies in its sectional response to the sloping site, which gives the centre an ambiguous scale and presents two distinct spatial experiences. From the courtyard, the centre appears domestically scaled, with a surprising translucency thanks to extensive glazing shaded by deep overhanging eaves. By contrast, its sheer 'thick wall' exterior appears almost impenetrable. Articulated by deep recesses, the façades are punctured by small windows angled at 45 degrees to provide sun control. Here, the roof is shallow pitched, ending abruptly at the wall's edge where it is traced by framed openings at eaves level. The materials – red brick, raw concrete and painted sheet metal – relate to those used throughout the main campus.

ADDRESS Francois Road, University of Natal, Cato Manor [25 D5]
CLIENT Education & Innovation Foundation
STRUCTURAL ENGINEER M E Masojada & Partners
CONTRACT VALUE R10 million
SIZE 3372 square metres
GETTING THERE travel west up Berea Road; turn left at Cleaver Road (which becomes Bulwer Road). Continue south on Bulwer Road, across MacDonald Road into Nicholson Road (island down its middle); proceed to next set of traffic lights and turn right into Francois Road. Travel west for approximately 2 kilometres until you reach Anniversary Avenue. Turn left into the university grounds. The building shares parking with the sports centre
ACCESS open

Durban, The Ridge

Hallen Custers Smith 1993

Durban, The Ridge

Hallen Custers Smith 1993

EPA offices

Wedged between suburbia and the western freeway into the city, this small building accommodates the architects' own office/studio and is one of a trio of related buildings on its 'buffer zone' site.

The challenges of its awkward siting have been exploited to generate an architecture of contrasts: the freeway is met with a solid exterior and eye-catching billboard; suburbia is embraced with a north-facing verandah and a courtyard on to which the building opens. Characteristically for the work of this practice, the building is presented as a composition of primary geometric forms articulated through variations in materials.

An indented entrance at the side provides access to a double-volume atrium and reception area – a protected space used to mediate between the building's two levels. Interior spaces are minimally defined through strategically positioned columns and screen walls.

Durban, The Ridge

ADDRESS 61 Ramsay Avenue, Musgrave [25 A7]
CLIENT Elphick Proome Architects
STRUCTURAL ENGINEER Martin & Associates
CONTRACT VALUE R500,000
SIZE 657 square metres
GETTING THERE Mynah bus to Tollgate
ACCESS by appointment (telephone 031 207 1414))

Elphick Proome Architects 1993

Elphick Proome Architects 1993

North Durban

TREE Education and Care Centre

The Association for Training and Resources in Early Education (TREE), was established in 1985 to support education and care centres throughout KwaZulu-Natal. Providing non-formal training programmes for administrators, staff and parents, it mobilises desperately needed resources, particularly within the poorer communities.

While serving as a model for TREE teachers and trainees from around the region, the centre is very much rooted in its context, serving the needs of children living in the neighbouring settlements. Moreover, it was built by unemployed local people who in the process were given an opportunity to acquire training and construction skills.

The design is a single-storey linear building with administration and classroom spaces on either side of a glazed internal street. Inside, the atmosphere is bright and airy, with the street opening to form a series of alcoves with 'windows' which allow trainees to observe classroom activities without distracting proceedings. Classrooms are sunken at a lower level to the street. On the classroom side of the building the roof overshoots the irregular plan to create a verandah space on to which the classrooms open. External walls are studded with jewel-like mosaics which, along with recycled furnishings made on the premises and the children's arts and crafts, result in a building full of colour, energy and creativity.

ADDRESS 69 Krishna Road, Riverside [20 A2]
CLIENT Association for Training and Resources in Early Education
STRUCTURAL ENGINEER L S C Brunette & Partners
CONTRACT VALUE R400,000 SIZE 460 square metres
GETTING THERE follow the Umgeni Road and take the old North Coast Road (R102). Turn into Krishna Road at the traffic lights; the centre is at the top of the hill on your right-hand side ACCESS open

North Durban

Liebenberg Masojada 1995

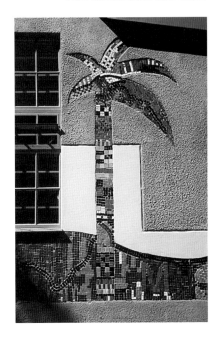

North Durban

Liebenberg Masojada 1995

'Terra Cruiser' and Ship House

Dookey Ramdarie was an affluent Indian bus builder with a taste for the unconventional. He was also a voracious traveller whose passion went beyond mere journeying: first, he created the 'Terra Cruiser', a home in the shape of an aeroplane poised for take-off above the valley. It has bedrooms in the wings, an undercarriage, a television room with row seats in the tail and, in the cockpit, a lounge with views to either side. (On seeing it, the pilot of an aircraft flying overhead once mistakenly reported that a plane had crashed in the middle of this Indian suburb.)

Ramdaari's next endeavour was the Ship House, sailing east out of Duffs Road Indian township, high on dry land about 15 kilometres from the coast. Even the offices and factory of the family business have their façade constructed out of real bus bodies. This piece of Pop architecture represents the resilience and desire for freedom, self-expression and eccentricity of many of those who suffered under apartheid.

ADDRESS 7 Starling Road (Terra Cruiser) and 20 Falcon Road (Ship House), Duffs Road township [7 D5]
CLIENT Dookey Ramdarie
GETTING THERE travel north on Umgeni Road. Continue northwards along the North Coast Road (R102) crossing over the Umgeni River, and proceed towards KwaMashu/Phoenix/Duffs Road. After approximately 6.5 kilometres you will reach Duffs Road township which is situated on the hillside to the left. The Terra Cruiser is unmissable as you approach ACCESS by appointment. For the Terra Cruiser contact Jay and Reena Ramdarie on 031 565 2250; for the Ship House contact Ashwin Ramdarie on 031 565 1632

North Durban

Dookey Ramdarie 1971–81

Dookey Ramdarie 1971–81

South Durban

Kwamanzini truck wash facility

Centred around existing facilities, this project provides improved conditions for railway workers who clean freight trains in 24-hour shifts. Its key element is a shed structure, 300 metres long and 17 metres wide, enclosing three parallel lines of tracks. Steel trusses, curved at one end, rhythmically modulate the shed's immense length, dividing it into 40 bays and tempering the huge mass by giving it a vaguely aerodynamic profile.

Gantries with retractable stairs allow overhead access for workers and equipment. The stairs are expressed externally on the vertical north-east elevation, their positions marked by a series of Y-shaped columns. These in turn are expressed as Y-shaped gaps in the horizontally ribbed cladding, a crisp incision making a bold pattern along the building's elevation. The elevated gantries run through these openings to connect with the external stairs and services. A narrow strip of translucent sheeting inserted in the roof of the canopy brings daylight into the tunnel-like interior.

Various facilities for the workers are clustered along the north-east side of the washing shed, the gap between forming a landscaped strip. An office, mess and wash building are arranged to create outdoor recreation areas shielded from the harsh conditions of the site.

ADDRESS Bay Head Road, Maydon Wharf [33 A8]
CLIENT Spoornet
PROJECT ARCHITECT Joy Brasler
STRUCTURAL ENGINEER John Mugglestone
CONTRACT VALUE R21 million
SIZE 5100 square metres square
GETTING THERE going south on old South Coast Road, turn left into Bay Head Road; the building is on the right, about 500 metres from the road
ACCESS ask at the gate to speak to the depot manager; office hours only

South Durban

Protekon 1997

Protekon 1997

Chatsworth Crematorium

A multi-denominational crematorium within the Chatsworth Cemetery, this building reflects in both its design and its landscaping the symbolic concept of 'progression' – the journey through life, and life after death.

From a northern entry point the complex steps to follow the site's gentle slope, maximising its orientation to the west (so that the setting sun becomes the backdrop to Hindu and Southern Indian cremations, which take place only in the afternoon/early evening). The arrangement consists of three pavilion-like modules, formalised by a simple axial geometry, radiating from a common service area in the south to public areas in the north. Service areas are concealed behind landscaped berms and roof gardens, while the public buildings, lightweight colonnaded gazebos, stand serenely at the head of ramped processional routes. Each pavilion has a distinctive geometric roof – a large dome for the centrally positioned main chapel, with a pyramid for the smaller chapels on either side of it. A smaller domed structure (the Hare Chandra, used during Tamil and Talago ceremonies) is placed in front of the main chapel. The main chapels are characterised by square plans, enclosed altars and sliding screens which offer some privacy. The Hare Chandra is completely exposed, with a centralised altar which overlooks a reflecting pool and a waterfall.

ADDRESS Chatsworth Crematorium, Mobeni Heights [39 A6]
CLIENT Architectural Division Durban Corporation, Port Natal – Ebhowe Joint Services Board
STRUCTURAL ENGINEER A Sankar & Associates
CONTRACT VALUE R4.5 million SIZE 958 square metres
GETTING THERE take the Higginson Highway (M1) turn-off from the South Coast Road (R102) travelling south. The cemetery is approximately 2 kilometres on your right from the exit ACCESS open

John Royal Architects 1994

South Durban

John Royal Architects 1994

Kwadengezi Cemetery reception area

This pavilion stands on the flat portion of a hill in the rural area of Kwadengezi. An off-shoot of a project to extend a graveyard down the slopes, its design responded to the community's request for an assembly area where they could gather and hear their minister preach before going to the graveyard itself. In black South African culture, funerals are big events, with the burial ritual sometimes lasting three or four days, and people often coming from far and wide to attend. Consequently, the brief also called for parking for cars, buses and taxis, wash facilities and an area for the ceremonial killing and cooking of animals.

The building – a simple roof structure of two suspended, triangular planes – is a powerful element in the landscape. It is built as a diagram, with robust, direct detailing. A curved screen wall with a central gap for access isolates the sheltered ceremonial space from the noise and activity of the parking area. Once inside, you feel part of the broader landscape. The flying roof seems almost incidental, its two structural beams reinforcing the path of the aisle, giving it a processional feel where it terminates in a podium for the coffin, totally open to the view of the valley beyond. For security reasons, nothing is removable (even the corrugated iron roof is held down with concrete).

ADDRESS Kwadengezi
CLIENT Ebodwhe Joint Services Board
STRUCTURAL ENGINEER M E Masojada & Partners
GETTING THERE Toll Road west. Take the Marionhill turn-off, keep left. You come eventually to the Nagina township turn-off to the right. Proceed, then take the left turn into Kwadengezi. This is the 'main road'; the cemetery is right at the end of the road
ACCESS open

South Durban

Liebenberg Masojada 1995

Liebenberg Masojada 1995

West Durban

Sherwood Jungle Nursery

This tropical garden nursery evokes the exotic imagery of vernacular Thai architecture. Quietly at home in Durban's tropical climate, it creates a wonderfully relaxing environment in which to browse for plants or simply take a stroll.

The nursery was built bit by bit on leased land designated for community use. Because of the uncertainty of the lease, its buildings were designed so that they could be easily unbolted and relocated if necessary. The centre has, however, proved a successful leisure facility and has won strong support from the local community.

The natural topography of the site consists of three level platforms terracing southwards. Occupying the middle section, the complex centres around a rectangular internal courtyard ringed by a double-storey sales pavilion which provides the entrance, two parallel open display pavilions, and a tea house at the end. The approach from the parking area leads up a gentle incline to the sales pavilion which acts both as a barrier to the harsh environment of the adjacent freeway and as a window on to the leafy oasis of the nursery beyond. The lush courtyard ramps down over two levels, a change accentuated by the continuous eave line of its flanking pavilions. At their lower levels large roof overhangs and verandahs emphasise the loose definition between outdoor and indoor spaces.

ADDRESS 814 Jan Smuts Highway, Sherwood [19 E5]
CLIENTS Jeremy Byrd and Wilfred Grey
CONTRACT VALUE R600,000
GETTING THERE travelling west on the N3 highway west, take Jan Smuts Highway (R613) exit. The complex is on your right next to Sherwood Sports Club
ACCESS open every day 8.30–17.00

West Durban

Colin Savage Architect 1992

West Durban

Colin Savage Architect 1992

KwaDhoti community hall and pre-school

Built to improve the informal settlement in the area known as KwaDhoti ('Place of Dirt'), this structure stands on steep land among upgraded shacks overlooking the Bissar Road landfill, the city dump. Here, as on the fringes of many developing, urbanising cities, the residents make a living mostly by scavenging from the landfill. Retrieving edible food, building materials, furniture or clothing, or carrying out formal and informal recycling work, are all part of the deal in KwaDhoti, as are the many health hazards associated with living and working there.

The centre serves not only the settlement but also the adjacent formal (predominantly Asian) residential area. The brief called for a hall to accommodate 200 people as well as pre-school facilities for 60 children. The design incorporates an entrance court and seating at the upper level approach with a playground area below contained by the main volume of the hall and the small, freestanding playroom buildings. Steel portals, a concrete frame and blockwork were used for the hall, with an impermanent iron sheeting and pole structure for the pre-school buildings. The scale and materials echo the surrounding dwellings.

ADDRESS Kennedy Road, Clare Hills [19 E5]
CLIENT Informal Settlements Division of the Urban Foundation (now disbanded)
CONTRACT VALUE R260,000 (total)
SIZE 250 square metres (hall); 165 square metres (pre-school)
GETTING THERE head out of Durban on the N2 towards the North Coast. Take the M19 along Umgeni Road, then the first right into Kennedy Road (just before the intersection of the N2 and the Umgeni River). Proceed and the centre is on your left ACCESS open

West Durban

Derek van Heerden Architect 1993

West Durban

Derek van Heerden Architect 1993

House Pattundeen

Part of the brief for this house was 'to create an appropriate environment to promote the quality of family life in both the community and spiritual sense…' Embodying values deeper than mere functionalism, the result reflects the influence of anthroposophy (the teachings of Rudolph Steiner), manifest in the organic forms which are sculptured to form a womb-like enclosure.

Arrival is a sequential experience, heightening the sense of transition from the bustle of the outside road to the tranquillity of the inner family sanctum. A portal at the main gate of the outer entrance court forms the first threshold and marks the way into an inner court. The portico roof over the front door announces the second entry threshold. Inside, the focal point is the Hindu prayer area – a place of calm that binds the whole. There are three radial zones: the formal lounge and dining area, the informal family area, and the bedrooms. Each space is given its particular ambiance through close attention to scale, materials and views.

Exterior forms derived from the growth patterns of lush vegetation are a conscious attempt to express a subtropical quality in the architecture.

ADDRESS 43A Jan Hofmeyer Road, Westville [17 E7]
CLIENT Mr Naren Pattenundeen
STRUCTURAL ENGINEER Nathoo & Associates
CONTRACT VALUE R1.5 million
SIZE 400 square metres
GETTING THERE take the St James (M32) off-ramp from the N3 highway travelling west. This leads directly into Jan Hofmeyer Road across the M13 highway
ACCESS by appointment through the architects (telephone 031 294 122)

West Durban

Johnson Murray Architects 1993

West Durban

Johnson Murray Architects 1993

Architects' offices

Next to an office development in the Pinetown CBD, the triangular building envelope for Myles Pugh Sherlock Murray's offices was predetermined by building lines and a servitude cutting diagonally through the site. The architects responded with a simple and economical design with strong visual impact.

A play of mass and transparency distinguishes the building's two separate functions (the architects' own offices on one side of a glazed service core, lettable space on the other). Both are held under a curved, wing-like roof structure – giving the building an extraordinary sense of weightlessness – reinforced by a dynamic support system comprising two diagonal steel columns supporting struts and hangers.

The main feature of the design is the elevation of the two-storey wing accommodating the architects' offices, which is suspended over the servitude. Its floor slab juts through the supporting columns, resting only on three points of support at ground level. Three external decks take advantage of views over the adjacent park.

The plan allows for natural cross-ventilation of all offices and the double-volume reception area. Air-conditioning is limited to small console units to assist during humid summer days.

ADDRESS 45 Sunnyside Lane, Pinetown
CLIENT Myles Pugh Sherlock Murray Architects
STRUCTURAL ENGINEER Ken Tucker Associates SIZE 500 metres square
GETTING THERE take the Old Main Road (M31) turn-off from Jan Smuts Highway (M13) travelling west. After approximately 4 kilometres turn right into Glenugie Road. Cross Kings Road, with the Sanlam Centre on your left-hand side. Turn right into Sunnyside Lane
ACCESS by appointment

West Durban

Myles Pugh Sherlock Murray 1995

Myles Pugh Sherlock Murray 1995

Durban, surrounding areas

Port Workers Facility, Richards Bay Harbour

A domestically scaled shelter is introduced on to the windswept plain of the Richards Bay port area, a tough environment of industrial-scale warehousing, concrete silos and overhead conveyors. Designed to provide improved conditions for port workers engaged in unloading and stacking goods from ships, it comprises two separate service buildings embracing a large garden court: one a linear block housing an administrative office, laundry, kitchens and toilets; the other a sensuous curved building providing shower and changing room facilities. Project architect Jeremy Steere describes the concept as 'perhaps a celebration of unity … the covered walkways being the arms linking the straight, orthogonal (Western) world to the sensuous, organic (African) world'. The metaphor is reiterated in the choice of materials: facebrick for the linear block, alluding to the adjacent industrial buildings and nearby residential suburbs; and, for the curved building, a rough-textured pigmented plaster reminiscent of the mud architecture of the area.

ADDRESS corner Petingo and Pegasus Roads, off Newark Road, Port of Richards Bay
PROJECT ARCHITECT Jeremy Steere
CLIENT Portnet (Port Authority)
CONTRACT VALUE R2.5 million
SIZE 1230 square metres
GETTING THERE travelling north on the N2 take the exit to Richards Bay. After approximately 8 kilometres turn off to the port. Turn left at the customs gate. The facility is next to the Visitors Centre
ACCESS by appointment; contact Port public relations on 0351 905 3118

Protekon 1997–98

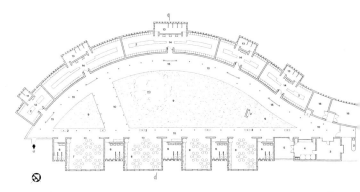

Durban, surrounding areas

Protekon 1997–98

Elywazini Visitors Centre (place of knowledge)

Like other post-democracy projects in South Africa's harbours, this had as its primary objective the design of a building that would manifest the Port Authority's new human ethos. It achieves this initially by the way in which its scale contrasts with the hard monolithic buildings surrounding it, and also by its formal modulation and its establishment of internal and external spaces of equal hierarchy. In this sense it is an inversion of previous typologies prevalent in harbour areas. It transforms materials traditionally used in harbour environments – corrugated aluminium sheeting, brown facebrick – to establish new associations of accessibility and welcome. Gum pole posts, timber rafters and stone flooring increase the sense of tactility, while the use of aluminium, stone and timber makes reference to the products exported from the port.

The building welds together two existing bunker-like office blocks by defining the previously overexposed courtyard space between them. A linear circulation route is manipulated along its length from entrance to foyer, to internal gathering space to external verandah. On the elevation facing the most hostile harbour environment, a linear exhibition space is clearly expressed as a protective, enclosing wall.

ADDRESS Ventura Road, Port of Richards Bay
CLIENT Portnet
STRUCTURAL ENGINEER Paruk and Associates
CONTRACT VALUE R1.4 million
GETTING THERE travelling north on the N2 take the exit to Richards Bay. After approximately 8 kilometres turn off to the port. Turn left at the customs gate. Opposite the huge silos
ACCESS by appointment; contact Port public relations (0351 905 3118)

Protekon 1996

Protekon 1996

House Williams

On a lonely hillside in rural Franklin, this fascinating house was built by and for a retired farmer and his wife. The brief required that the fabric should be materials recycled from the farmer's nearby deserted parental home and trading store, and that the process itself use as little energy as possible. Consequently, its 9-metre-high structure is a combination of sandstone, old bricks, traditional timber and thatch with railway sleepers sourced for door and window frames (and for kitchen cupboards). A car windscreen set in the thick thatched roof provides a skylight. The massive, oval-planned house gently blends in with its surroundings and, like its beautifully landscaped garden, looks like it has always been there.

The most important feature of the design is a trombe wall which occupies a huge section of the north elevation. It comprises two layers: an outer skin lined on one side with tin foil which opens up on a counterweight; and, within the wall, big drums of sump oil behind a perspex sheet. These are heated by the reflection of the sun off the tin during the day. At sunset the wall is closed and the captured energy heats the house by convection. To heat the lounge you simply walk to the corner where there is an old jam tin, open the lid and warm air rises up. The system has been sensational – creating a comfortable place to live in a very cold area at little cost.

ADDRESS 'Braeside', Franklin
CLIENT Bobby and Judi Williams
SIZE 310 square metres
GETTING THERE take the N2 south. Turn right at Kokstad, drive through the town on the R167 towards Franklin; 6 kilometres beyond Franklin, take a left turn (at a derelict store) on to the dirt road. Braeside lies among the trees on your right-hand side about 4 kilometres up this road
ACCESS by appointment; contact the clients on 0374 7474 691

Harber Masson Associates 1994

Harber Masson Associates 1994

Gamalakhe College of Education

Gamalakhe is a fairly recent village designed in the Bantustan tradition – as a dormitory town for Margate and Port Shepstone. But it has started to have a life of its own with many substantial houses, schools and community facilities. The site chosen for this teacher-training college is the most exquisite, prominent and precious piece of land in the vicinity – a tabletop peninsula towering over deep valleys with views over hills and glimpses of the sea.

Access to the campus is via a narrow saddle which separates the town from the college entrance gates and sweeps through an avenue of trees, hugging the contour around the earth berm of the sports field, before it swings west on to the main axis between administration and residential accommodation. These two functions are compressed in fragmented, parallel layers that wrap around the edge of the site. On their inner side, the L-shaped wings cup the large academic courtyard which binds the major campus components and serves as the arrival point serving both the public and students. The organisation of the lecture blocks, recreation field and central refectory is skewed to the main wings, jutting forward so that the large space is broken into two tapering interconnected sections.

The main arrival court funnels towards the library, the focus of the campus taking pride of place at the pivotal corner junction of the wings. With an expansive terrace, this commands the most spectacular views of the region. Its entrance, as with those of the student halls and lecture theatre, is articulated by totem-pole-like columns that extend its structure to encroach into the court space. Brick steps set against the grey paving of the courtyard provide further definition. Continuity is provided by the extensive use of smooth red facebrick, cool white roof sheeting and the continuous series of arcades that flank the teaching spaces. Breaks

Architects Collaborative 1997

Architects Collaborative 1997

between the teaching buildings become gateways into the residential domain via lounges, supervisor accommodation and offices.

The design of the residence buildings underlines the image of a citadel. Forming a crown to the plateau, their bastion walls shelter secluded residential courtyards within, while providing openings to the dramatic views beyond from common rooms and private group lounges.

Through its communal garden courts, this project consciously dissolves the boundary between 'day campus' (classrooms) and 'night campus' (residences), creating an intimate relationship between study, recreation and private living spaces. Despite this fluidity, individual and group privacy is achieved by the clear definition of terrain so that each operates independently. Explicit in this design is the positive development of community life and the added wish that this new institution be pushed beyond the academic calendar and be made available as a resource to the rest of the province.

ADDRESS Gamalahke Village
CLIENT Province of Kwazulu-Natal Department of Works
STRUCTURAL ENGINEER VKE Engineers
CONTRACT VALUE R50 million
SIZE 20,000 square metres
GETTING THERE drive down the South Coast Road through Port Shepstone; turn right at the Country Club Golf Course at Shelly Beach, cross over the bridge over the highway (approximately 20 kilometres) turn left at the petrol station in town; follow the ring road southwards and after approximately 3.5 kilometres, check signs, turn off to your left-hand side
ACCESS announce yourself

Architects Collaborative 1997

Architects Collaborative 1997

Index

South Africa: a guide to recent architecture

South Africa: a guide to recent architecture

South Africa: a guide to recent architecture

South Africa: a guide to recent architecture

South Africa: a guide to recent architecture

South Africa: a guide to recent architecture

All photographs are by Andreas Werner
    and Christina Muwanga except:
page 79 Alfio Torrisi Architect
page 121 Stefan Antoni Architect
page 163 Meyer Pienaar Archs & Urban
    Designers
page 169 Ove Arup Associates
page 185 Harold H Le Roith Architects
pages 187, 89 Peter Rich Architect
pages 195, 197 Stephen Le Roith
    Architects
pages 199, 223,225, 227 Jo Noero
    Architect
page 201 Julius and Company
page 221 Keeves Styne Inc. (Soweto
    Station Upgrades)
page 237 Conservation Corporation
page 247 Design Workshop
page 249 Myles Pugh Sherlock and
    Murray
page 285 Stauch Vorster Architects
pages 301, 311 Liebenberg Masojada
page 319 Johnson Murray Architects
pages 325, 327 Protekon
page 329 Harber Masson Associates
pages 331, 333 Architects Collaborative